HANDBOOK

FOR

NEW BELIEVERS

Rev. David R. Wallis

VERSION 1.0

"Handbook for New Believers"

All Scripture quotations used in this book are from the *King James Version Bible* unless otherwise stated.

Reprinted May, 2010 in
the United States of America

ISBN # 1-59665-030-3

For more information, please contact:
Zion Christian Publishers
A *Zion Fellowship*® Ministry
P.O. Box 70
Waverly, New York 14892

Phone: 607-565-2801
Toll free: 1-877-768-7466
Fax: 607-565-3329
www.zionfellowship.org

ACKNOWLEDGMENTS

We wish to extend our thanks to all the following:

- To Betsy Caram – the general editor of this book. For your overall input into the flow of this book, as well as the many hours spent in editing the content of *Handbook for New Believers*.
- To Mary Humphreys – for her valuable editorial suggestions and assistance in the proofing of this book.
- To Tonya Coursey – for her diligence behind the computer, as she transcribed tapes of classes into manuscript form.
- To my wife Marilyn – for her assistance in transcribing tapes and proofing this book.
- To Carla Borges and Sarah Kropf – for their cooperative effort in the excellent design of the front cover of this book.
- To Justin Kropf – for the "final touches" in the proofreading of this book, as well as the formatting of this manuscript.

Dedicated

To the Lord Jesus Christ, the Captain of our salvation, who came to seek and to save that which was lost.

and

To Dr. Brian J. Bailey my teacher at Bible college, and spiritual father, whose godly life has been such a role model to me, and whose ministry has inspired me to "press toward the mark for the prize of the high calling of God in Christ Jesus."

and

To Marilyn my dear wife and best friend, who has helped and encouraged me so much in the production of this book.

Contents

Introduction

GUIDELINES FOR GROWTH

Throughout this handbook, volume number one, you will find many keys that will help you mature in your Christian life. These *guidelines for growth* are essential truths that you will need to sustain you as you continue on in the Lord. From beginning to end, you will see repeatedly that the most important key for your personal growth as a new Christian is your knowledge of the Word of God. This is vital for all new believers, for as it says in Psalm 119:105, His Word is truly *"a lamp unto our feet, and a light unto our path."*

In many ways, serving God requires the discipline and stamina of an athlete, and the path is not always easy. Therefore, in order to prepare you completely, we will share many important truths that will assist you as a new believer. For example, one of the important spiritual truths that is covered in this handbook is the importance of water baptism, because this act of obedience is an outward sign of what is happening inwardly in your heart. The Word of God commands us to be water baptized. Matthew 28:19-20 tells us: *"Go therefore and make disciples of all the nations, baptizing them in the name of the Father and of the Son and of the Holy Spirit, teaching them to observe all things that I have commanded you"* (NKJV).

We will also explore the subject of deliverance. Deliverance occurs within you when God's power breaks the bondages in your life, and sets you free from evil spirits that perhaps came down to you from past generations (Num. 14:18). God wants to set the captives free. In fact, Jesus came to set you completely free! The Word of God makes that clear when it says, *"If the Son therefore shall make you free, ye shall be free indeed"* (John 8:36).

In this study, much will be spoken about the Holy Spirit. The Holy Spirit is so very important to us, for He is actually the third person of the Godhead. There is One God, but three persons in the Godhead who are the Father, Son, and Holy Spirit. While this is a great mystery of God, it is not difficult to understand if you have faith in God's Word.

There is also a natural example that will help you understand this enigma. If you heat water to boiling point it will become steam, but at room temperature that same water would be a clear, cool liquid. Yet if you lower the temperature to freezing, that water becomes ice. However, in all these forms, it is still water, or H_2O. In other words, it is the same chemical formula, but in three different forms. In the same way, the Trinity of God shows us three aspects of the personality of God: God the Father, God the Son, and God the Holy Spirit. John 14:26 declares that the Holy Spirit is sent from God: *"But the Helper, the Holy Spirit, whom the Father will send in My name, He will teach you all things."* The Holy Spirit is important because He will help you understand what the heart of God is trying to show you in His Word.

We will also encourage you to receive the baptism in the Holy Spirit, which includes the evidence of speaking with other tongues. This experience will give you power and boldness to be a witness for Christ. It will prepare and enable you to serve God with all of your strength, and also with His power and anointing in your life. On the day of Pentecost as the Holy Spirit was poured out, people cried, *"What shall we do?"* When Peter gave the answer, he said, *"Repent!"* (Acts 2:37-38). When you made the decision to accept Christ, and said "yes" to Him in your heart, that is exactly what happened to you. You repented and were saved, and now your name is written in the Book of Life. Yet as you grow and mature in faith and in the knowledge of Jesus Christ, there is much more that is required for you to do as a new believer. These steps will also be covered in this handbook.

Additional subjects not included in this edition but equally important to you as a new believer will be covered in our sequel to this book, which is entitled ***Further Steps for New Believers***. In that book we will stress the importance of praise and worship in your new life. Worshipping God brings you into His presence, and it is there that you are changed and transformed into His image.

The second volume will also cover in depth the subject of tithing, which is an essential part of your new Christian life. We will discuss the difference between a tithe and an offering, while giving many scriptural examples that reveal God's heart and desire to bless you in this important matter.

In God's eyes, the family is the very foundation of the Church and society. Therefore, we have included within this second volume, valuable keys to help you as a new believer to come into God's divine order in the important area of family relationships. In these last days, God's heart is to bring restoration to the family. His desire is to *"turn the heart of the fathers to the children, and the heart of the children to their fathers"* (Mal. 4:5-6). We will also discuss the relationship of husband and wife, while giving much scriptural evidence of God's desire to keep marriages together.

Further Steps for New Believers will also detail the Scriptural facts regarding the Second Coming of Christ. As a new believer, you will need to be prepared for His coming; our study is intended to help you live in the light of this reality and for eternity.

We therefore commend to you the study of these two volumes—***Handbook for New Believers*** and ***Further Steps for New Believers***. It is our prayer that through them the God of all grace will *"establish, strengthen, and settle* *you"* (1 Pet. 5:10). As you gain insight into the deeper things of God and increase in knowledge and discernment, it is also our hope that the Holy Spirit will guide your feet upon a good path, as you have just begun your exciting, but sometimes difficult, journey unto Christian perfection.

Chapter One

Starting the Christian Life

JESUS CAME TO GIVE YOU LIFE

Your decision to choose Christ, turn from your sin, and ask Jesus into your heart is the most important decision you will ever make. Therefore, this handbook for new believers is written with the purpose of helping you get established in the basics of the Christian life, so that when Satan comes around like a roaring lion, he will not be able to thwart God's wonderful plan of salvation. The Lord spoke to mankind in John 10:10 that He had come to give life, and life more abundant. This then is His purpose in your life. He wants to give you peace, rest, joy, and a more abundant life as you continue to live for Him.

On the other hand, your adversary Satan will try everything to [illegible] continuing on with your commitment to follow [illegible] complacent, to go back into sin, to backslide, and to get separated from God. However, by following the foundational truths contained in God's Word, you can learn how to defeat him. It is with this thought in mind that we have compiled this new believer's handbook. Our prayer is that it will be a source of strength to you as you seek to follow Christ.

THE NEW BIRTH EXPERIENCE

When a baby is born, he cannot be left alone and unattended. Everyone knows that a newborn baby is unable to properly care for himself. The newborn must be fed, changed, bathed, and completely protected. As it is in the natural, we see this same truth in the spiritual realm. When you are *"born again"* into Christ, you need to be taken care of, protected, and fed the right kind of spiritual diet. Thus another purpose of this handbook for new believers is to give proper instruction to you regarding the right kind of spiritual nourishment, food that will not only protect and feed you but will also cause your soul to prosper in Christ.

WHAT DOES IT MEAN TO BE SAVED?

Many things happen when you become a Christian, and there is really no one way to adequately describe the experience. The Bible speaks of this transformation in many different ways. One of the familiar words that the Bible often uses is *"saved."* In Acts 2:21 we read: *"Whosoever shall call on the name of the Lord shall be saved."* What does it mean to be saved? Simply stated, it means that you are saved from something. You are saved from hell. Just as heaven is a real place, hell is likewise a real place.

The Bible tells us that hell is a place of weeping, wailing, and gnashing of teeth; Jesus repeatedly warns us to keep out of it. In fact, Jesus spoke more about hell than He did about heaven. Jude 1:13 speaks about hell as *"the blackness of darkness forever."* In Ezekiel, hell is described as a place that is under the earth. We know a number of people who have either been to hell or have seen visions of hell; it is a place of horrible darkness. There is a book written by Mary Baxter called *A Divine Revelation of Hell*. It describes her experience of being in hell for a period of thirty nights. Jesus went with her into hell, where she saw many formidable scenes and talked with people whose eternal dwelling place was in this place of darkness.

Dr. Brian J. Bailey has also had visions of hell. At one time, he was actually taken to hell where he met one of the former kings of England who was surrounded by such darkness that he cried out to him, "Show me the way." There is no second chance after a person dies. The Word of God tells us clearly in Hebrews 9:27 that it is *"**appointed** unto men once to die, but after this the judgment."* The good news, however, is that you can be saved from hell! When you become a Christian, you are "saved;" you can be sure that you are saved because Jesus has come into your heart.

The Bible also speaks of this experience of being saved as being "born again." Being a Christian and being saved means that you are given a new birth. Jesus, in John's Gospel, chapter three, talks to a man whose name was Nicodemus. He was a religious man, a Pharisee, a ruler of the Jews, and a member of the Sanhedrin, which was the highest Jewish council in the first century.

When he saw all the miracles that Jesus did, it caused him to say, *"No one can do these signs that You do unless God is with him."* He was undoubtedly wondering, "How can this man do all these miracles?" Jesus then replied, *"You must be born again."* Nicodemus was confused, as he asked Jesus, *"How can a man go back into his mother's womb and be born a second time?"* Jesus' reply is recorded for us in John 3:5: *"Verily, verily, I say unto thee, Except a man be born of water and of the Spirit, he cannot enter into the kingdom of God."*

This was a comparison between natural birth and spiritual birth. When a baby is born in the natural, the mother's water breaks right before the baby is born. In essence, this describes what it means to be born of water. Yet Jesus tells us in John's Gospel that we must be born a second time. Actually, what He is really saying is that there must be a spiritual birth into the kingdom of God that takes place within us. We must be born of the Spirit. This is what happens when a person turns from his sin and accepts Jesus into his heart. When you said yes to Jesus and prayed a sincere prayer asking Him to be your Savior, you were "born again." Now you are "born again" by the Spirit of God, yet it is not a natural birth but a spiritual one.

Being Transformed

An additional word that the Bible uses for being saved is "transformed." When you accept Jesus into your heart, you are transformed. The Bible says in 2 Corinthians 5:17, *"Therefore, if anyone is in Christ, he is a **new creation**; old things have passed away; behold, all things have become new"* (NKJV). When you are in Christ, you are a new creation. Therefore, old things have passed away (are passing away), and all things have become (are becoming) new. In other words, you have been and will be transformed by the Spirit of God.

Being Converted

As a new Christian, you will often hear the word "converted." Jesus said in Matthew 18:3, *"Unless you are **converted** and become as little children, you will by no means enter the kingdom of heaven"* (NKJV). To be converted means, "to turn around." You were going in one direction, but now you are converted and you are going in the opposite direction. When you are converted, the way you live and act is changed.

The word "justified" is also an important word that is used to describe your new Christian experience. To justify someone means to exonerate, pardon, or excuse him. Justified is a legal term, but in spiritual terminology it simply means, "just as if you had never sinned."

This is how God looks at you now, as you are set to begin your new life in Christ. Since the day you were born, God has kept a record of every sin that you have ever committed, even those sins that you have kept hidden from everyone else. It is important to realize that God has all these sins written down in a book.

At the moment of your conversion, when you recognized that Jesus died for you and all your sins were placed upon Him, at that moment you were justified. In other words, when you became a Christian, God looked again at your record of sins and He did not simply put a line through those sins, He blotted them out and washed them away completely with His own blood. You are now completely justified (exonerated, pardoned, excused) in His sight.

In Isaiah 1:18, we read: *"Come now, and let us reason together, saith the LORD: though your sins be as scarlet, they shall be as white as snow; though they be red like crimson, they shall be as wool."* Now when God looks at your name, there is nothing but a blank space where the record of your sin had been. Everything has been erased and forgiven, for you have now been "justified."

Being Reconciled

For an even deeper understanding, let us also look at the word "reconcile." When there is a war going on between two people, there is a wall between them, or a barrier. This was exactly your situation before you accepted Christ. This wall separated you from the goodness and mercy of God, but when you accepted Him this wall was broken down. You were separated from God when you were in sin because your sin made you an enemy with God. However, when Jesus died on the cross, His sacrifice gave you access to God. Therefore, your sins are now forgiven and you are reconciled back to God. You can now become friends with God, for there is no longer a separation. Ephesians 2:16 says, *"And that He might reconcile them both to God in one body through the cross, thereby putting to death the enmity"* (NKJV).

Summary

We have briefly defined six different words (that basically say the same thing) to explain what it means to become a Christian. These words are as follows:

1.) Saved
2.) Born Again
3.) Transformed
4.) Converted
[illegible]
[illegible]

While these terms are fundamentally different aspects of your salvation experience, each aspect is equally important to help you understand the depth of the love of God toward you. With each new step you take in Christ, whether you falter, fail, or succeed, you will need to meditate upon the truths of Scripture concerning our wonderful salvation, which speaks so convincingly of God's faithfulness. For a light (which only comes from God) has now been turned on in your being, dispelling the darkness that in times past has separated you from God's holy and righteous presence.

Therefore, our prayer is that more and more you would desire to know every aspect of His mercy and grace so that you will grow and prosper in your walk with God. This is also our purpose for writing this handbook, for our desire is that you would walk in newness of life with your Savior, the Lord Jesus Christ.

WHAT DOES IT MEAN TO BE A CHRISTIAN?

A Christian is not just someone who understands Christian doctrine. Understanding with your mind what it means to be a Christian does not make you a Christian! The Bible tells us in James 2:19 that the demons also believe, and tremble. If you desire to be a real Christian, it is not enough just to believe. A Christian is not someone who simply tries to base his behavior on the ethics taught by Jesus in Matthew 7:12, which says: *"Therefore, whatever you want men to do to you, do also to them, for this is the Law and the Prophets"* (NKJV).

This passage describes the Golden Rule—"do unto others as you would have them do unto you." Just because you try to be good, and do good things (such as help the poor or do good works or good deeds), this does not make you a Christian. You cannot earn your salvation; you cannot work for it; you cannot pay for it!

Nor is a Christian someone who simply observes rites and ceremonies. When I was a baby, I was "christened" or "baptized" when the priest poured a few drops of water on my head. However, that did not make me a Christian—simply because I went through some ritual or ceremony. To be a Christian, you need to be of an age of understanding and accountability. You need to repent of your sin, and sincerely ask Jesus into your heart as your Savior and Lord. Remember that Jesus said you must be "born again."

Therefore, a Christian is someone who recognizes that he has rebelled against God and, because of that, deserves to be punished. We all deserve punishment for our sins. If a person robs a bank and is caught, a judge requires him to pay the penalty for that transgression. If we break the law, [illegible] [illegible]

In the same way as this thief has broken the law, we too have rebelled against God and therefore deserve to be punished. The Bible tells us that *"all have sinned and come short of the glory of God"* (Rom. 3:23).

WHY ARE WE CALLED SINNERS?

What makes you and me sinners? When we sin, does this in fact make us sinners? Or are we already a sinner, and therefore this is the reason that we sin? In actuality, from the day we are born we are sinners. Why? Not because of anything we have done, but because Adam, our first forefather, sinned. As a result of Adam's transgression, sin was brought into the world. No matter where we are from or what our skin color is, because we are descendents of Adam, we are born sinners. Simply stated, we sin because we are sinners. In other words, we all have a sin nature within us, and we are all born into iniquity. This is why we need a Savior.

Because I am a sinner and because I have sinned, I could never qualify to die for your sins. You in turn cannot die for my sins because you are also a sinner. Therefore, Jesus the sinless One had to come and take our place. He was born of a virgin, and He lived a sinless life as the pure and spotless Son of God. In fact, He was the only perfect human being who ever lived and that is why He could die for our sins on the cross. We are all sinners; the wages (or penalty) of sin is death (Rom. 6:23). Therefore, because God is a just God, He must punish us.

This punishment means that we deserve separation from God and a place in hell forever and ever. Yet God's will is that everyone should be saved from hell. God created hell for the devil and the fallen angels, not for us. It is for our redemption that Jesus died on the cross. He took the punishment we deserved upon Himself. He became a curse for us so that we could be free from the curse of the law (Gal. 3:13). He took our place so that when we turn from sin and ask Jesus into our hearts, we can be saved, born again, transformed, converted, justified, and reconciled to Him.

This basic rebellious instinct of mankind is what the Bible calls "sin." Scripture also tells us that sin is transgression of the Law (1 John 3:4). The Bible refers to the Law as the Ten Commandments and God requires us to follow them.

TURNING YOUR BACK ON SIN

As we have already said, a Christian is someone who believes that Jesus died for him on the cross and that He has taken the punishment we deserve. First Peter 3:18 tells us: *"For Christ also suffered once for sins, the just for the unjust, that He might bring us to God, being put to death in the flesh but made alive by the Spirit"* (NKJV). Furthermore, a Christian is one who has responded to God's call to turn from his acts [illegible] [illegible] his mind.

The Prodigal Son was living in sin, and he was living totally for himself. He was wasting all of his inheritance on prostitutes and riotous living but then he came to the end of himself, turned his back on sin, and declared his intention to return to his father's house. He purposefully began to walk in a new direction. This is an excellent example to us of true repentance. Instead of going your own way and living in sin, you turn around and follow Jesus. In your heart and mind you determine to walk in God's way and you decide to follow God's Word and God's Law. In essence, it is a change of heart and mind.

A Christian is also someone who has handed his life over to the Lord Jesus Christ. The Bible says that when you turn from sin, you become a new creation. Consequently, you become a child of God. You become part of the family of God, and God becomes your Father. Now you no longer simply know *about* God, you have the opportunity to know God for yourself. John 1:12 tells us: *"But as many as received him, to them gave he power to become the sons of God, even to them that believe on his name."*

CHRIST'S BLOOD HAS SET YOU FREE!

As a new believer, you are now able to partake of so many blessings in Christ. The first important blessing is freedom from guilt. As you get to know God in a personal way, you will find that He longs to set you free from the guilt in your life. Even without a Bible or without going to Church, God made us in such a way that everyone realizes instinctively when certain things we do are wrong. For example, we know in our heart that it is wrong to steal and to murder because we have a conscience. Therefore, when we violate our conscience, there is guilt which no counselor or psychologist can take away. The only thing that can remove this guilt of sin is the blood of Jesus Christ—for there is power in His blood. Hebrews 9:22 tells us: *"And according to the law almost all things are purified with blood, and without **shedding of blood** there is no remission"* (NKJV).

There is no remission of sin and there is no forgiveness without the blood of Jesus. Therefore, if you truly repent of your sins, they are washed away forever. Psalm 103:12 makes this clear when it says, ***"As far as the east is from the west,*** *So far has He removed our transgressions from us"* (NKJV). To explain the importance of this verse and its true meaning, there is an excellent natural example. If you are at the North Pole, you are able to travel and come to the South Pole. However, if you begin traveling east trying to reach the west, you never get to the western part because you are in fact always going east. Through this simple illustration, you can see that God willingly and completely gives all of us a new start. Micah 7:19 gives us a further proof of God's unwavering [illegible] [illegible] *into the depths of the sea"* (NKJV).

Does this mean that you are perfect overnight? Of course not! We are all born with a sinful nature, but when Christ comes into our hearts we receive His new nature. This sinful or old nature might be referred to as a "pig nature." Pigs are considered to be unclean animals because they love to be outside in the dirt and mud. They are comfortable in the muck and mire of life. Suppose we decided to bring that pig in the house and clean him up, give him a bath, put pretty clothes on him, and perhaps some sweet-smelling perfume. Will this change his natural instincts or his nature? No! Sooner or later, when the door is left open, this pig will go out and find the dirtiest, muddiest place he can find to roll around in as he squeals out in delight, "Aha, home sweet home!" This is the nature of a pig, which is like our old sinful nature.

In contrast to a pig, when a sheep falls into the mud, he does not like it at all and he will quickly climb out. It is the same with us when we sin. In your Christian walk, you will still at times make mistakes and sin. However, because you have the new nature of Christ within you, like a sheep you will want to get out of the mud (sin) quickly. As soon as possible, confess your sin to the Lord, tell Him you are sorry, and ask for His forgiveness. You can be assured that God promises to forgive and cleanse you from all unrighteousness (1 John 1:9).

HOW CAN YOU REALLY BE SURE YOU ARE A CHRISTIAN?

When you became a Christian, you were transferred from the domain of darkness into the Kingdom of God. However, your former master Satan is the prince of this earth, and his desire is for you to backslide and turn back to the old life. We have therefore included six ways that you can be assured that you are truly a Christian. They are as follows:

1.) YOU BECOME A TARGET OF SATAN: One of the first evidences that you are truly a Christian is that you quickly become a target of Satan. Because you have received God's free gift of salvation, Satan knows that now he has lost control over you. Consequently, every chance he gets he will attack you. In fact, he has become your greatest enemy and he will do anything to stop you from living for the Lord.

One of the foremost ways he attacks you is to cause doubt in your mind about your salvation. Often he tempts you to think such thoughts as "I am not really saved. I am just the same as I always was before!" However, this is not your own mind thinking these thoughts, but rather it is Satan planting these thoughts within you in order to cause discouragement and even retreat. Unfortunately, many Christians believe the doubts that Satan brings upon them instead of confessing only that which comes from God. During these times of doubt, however, you should be quoting the Word of God back to your adversary instead of giving in to his tactics.

Even Jesus the Son of God was tempted by the devil in the wilderness after He had fasted for forty days. Satan said to Jesus, *"**If** you be the Son of God!"* (Matt. 4:3-6, Luke 4:3-9).

In Jesus' time of struggle and temptation, the devil was trying to put doubt in His mind. Yet Jesus confidently replied, quoting from Deuteronomy 8:3, *"It is written, man shall not live by bread alone, but by every word that proceeds from the mouth of God"* (Matt. 4:4, NKJV). Jesus overcame the enemy by quoting the Word of God.

These same doubts overpowered Eve when Satan came to her in the garden. Eve knew that she and Adam were allowed to eat of every tree in the garden except the tree of good and evil. Yet Satan came to her and was able to cast doubts in her mind as he said, "Has God said…?" As a result, Eve fell and then Adam followed her into the transgression. This is why it is so important for you as a new believer to know the Bible.

When doubts come into your mind about your salvation, by knowing God's Word you will realize that these thoughts and doubts are from the enemy. You can then refuse them by saying, "I rebuke you, Satan, and I thank you, Jesus, that I am a child of God. Your Word says in 1 John 5:12, *'He that has the Son has (eternal) life.'* I believe Your Word. I thank You, Lord. I know I am a Christian!"

When Satan comes in like a flood with doubts, fears, and confusion, you are able through your study and meditation of the Bible to believe the facts of the Word of God. Therefore, any growth in your Christian life is dependent upon your knowledge of the Word of God. If you do not read the Word and feed upon it daily, you will simply not grow. Nor will you develop and mature in your Christian life.

2.) PEOPLE ATTACK YOU: When not only Satan attacks you but also others, this is another good indication that you have become a Christian. For example, some people may accuse you of pride when you tell them that you are a child of God and you know for sure that you are going to heaven. This often happens when the people around you do not know what it truly means to be a Christian. Actually, there are many people who attend Church, but they do not know whether they are saved. They have no assurance when they die that they will go to heaven.

As a new Christian, you are to trust in God's promises, for when you truly believe His promises you are given hope, strength, and courage. You can be certain that Jesus is in your heart because that is His promise to you in Revelation 3:20. *"Behold, I stand at the door, and knock: if any man hear my voice, and open the door, I will come in to him, and will sup with him, and he with me."* You can be sure that you have eternal life because you have Christ in you. First John 5:11-13 says, *"And this is the record, that God hath given to us eternal life, and this life is in his Son. He that hath the Son hath life; and he that hath not the Son of God hath not life. These things have I written unto you that believe on the name of the Son of God; that ye may* ***know*** *that ye have eternal life, and that ye may believe on the name of the Son of God."*

3.) YOU HAVE THE COURAGE TO TELL OTHERS: If as the Scripture says you believe and are persuaded, you need to tell your friends and family that you are following Jesus and going on with God. You cannot be a secret Christian. It does not matter if you do not know all the answers. The most important thing is that you know Jesus has come into your heart, and if you die you will go to heaven because your sins have been forgiven.

Actually, you are much like the blind man that was healed by Jesus in John 9:25. In this particular healing, there was a dispute with the Pharisees because Jesus chose to heal the man on the Sabbath day, an activity forbidden by those who interpreted the Jewish law. The man, however, could only exclaim, *"Whether He is a sinner or not I do not know. One thing I know: that though I was blind, now I see."* Now that you are saved, you can say the same thing: "I was blind but now I see! I was once lost and going to hell, but now I am saved. Now I am born again. Therefore, I will trust in God's promises because He is a holy and righteous God, and He cannot lie."

4.) THERE WILL BE A SIGNIFICANT CHANGE IN YOUR ATTITUDE: As we have already said, when you become a Christian you are a new creation. Therefore, others expect to see new attitudes developing in your life. Obviously, this does not happen overnight. However, if you pray and read the Word of God there will be a change of attitude. You will see a change in your ability to discern what is right and wrong. Your whole lifestyle will begin to change because of the Word of God. The more you begin to see God as a loving Father, the more you will then begin to have a deep-seated hatred for sin.

5.) YOU HAVE A GROWING LOVE FOR OTHER CHRISTIANS: When you were born again you were adopted into the family of God. Our Christian family will actually be our family for all eternity. Therefore, we should have a desire in our hearts to be with them. On the other hand, there should not be a desire to be with people who are opposing God or partaking of the world's evil ways. There should be a turning from that lifestyle. Proverbs 13:20 tells us: *"He who walks with wise men will be wise, But the companion of fools will be destroyed."* It is a fact that bad company corrupts good character. If a bad apple is in with good apples, what happens? They all turn bad. In the same way, when you surround yourself with bad friends, you too will become like them. So beware, new believer, and choose your friends wisely.

6.) THERE WILL BE AN INNER WITNESS IN YOUR OWN HEART: In this list, numbers one through five have dealt with outward things, but number six is quite different. When you have this inward witness, you will have a deepening conviction that God is your Father and that you are His child. In Romans 8:16, the Word tells us that: *"The Spirit Himself bears witness with our spirit that we are children of God."*

We all like to feel the presence of God. Sometimes the presence of God will be so real that you can feel Him very close to you. Sometimes you may be "slain in the Spirit," which is because of the power of the Holy Spirit that comes upon you and causes you to fall down. When you experience these things, you feel God's presence in a very tangible way; this is all very wonderful. However, you cannot live by these feelings. You cannot depend upon your feelings to determine whether you are saved or not. You must depend upon the fact of God's Word.

Obviously, it should be more normal for a Christian to feel God's presence than not to feel His presence, but it is dangerous to believe that God is there only because you feel Him. The fact that you do not feel Him also does not mean He has left you. Jesus promised that He would never leave or forsake you (Matt. 28:20). Your feelings and emotions go up and down. They change like the weather, which can be sunny or rainy, hot or cold. However, your feelings are not trustworthy indicators of your right standing with God.

An illustration of this would be an old steam train. The first car of the train is the engine, the second car is the tinder that holds the coal, and the third car is the carriage that carries the passengers. The first two are essential for the train to function. However, the third car is not essential.

Now let us compare this illustration to fact, faith, and feelings. The engine is like the ***fact*** of God's Word and the coal tinder is like ***faith*** that makes the fact of God's Word a reality within us. However, ***feelings*** are like the carriage—they are good to have but in no way essential in the operation of the facts of God's Word.

It is therefore important for a Christian to realize that feelings depend upon fact and faith, not the other way around. As a new believer, if you have fact and faith, you are like a man walking a high, narrow wall. If he keeps his eye on the wall he will not fall. But if he turns around, what will happen? He will fall. So the conclusion of the matter is this: you are always to look at the fact of what God says. If you depend instead upon your feelings, you will take your eyes off God's Word, which then gives an entrance for Satan to come in and try to make you fall by losing your faith. Stay focused, have faith, and believe God's Word, for this is how you will know with assurance that you are truly a child of God.

WHAT HAPPENS WHEN WE FAIL?

You may think that when you become a Christian you are expected to be perfect straightaway. However, it will not take you too long to realize that this is not the case. Along comes a test which you fail miserably, and you find yourself saying, "Now what do I do?" Then there is the temptation to quit. However, when you fail you must confess your sin and ask God to cleanse you by His blood (1 John 1:9). You must also be willing in your heart to change. You cannot just say, "God forgive me" and then keep doing what is wrong, for if you continue in this behavior there will come a time when you could lose your salvation.

We know from the Word of God that our names are written in the Lamb's Book of Life. However, if a person goes back to the world and deliberately keeps sinning, there comes a point where his name is taken out of this Book (Rev. 13:8; 17:8; 22:19; 3:5). Your salvation is secure as long as you continue on in the Lord, but if you deliberately go back to the world you can lose it. Therefore, it must be your heart's desire to please God and go God's way.

Babies fall down many times as they are learning to walk. In the same way, it takes time and persistence to become a strong and mature Christian. However, you will become strong as long as you keep going on, with trust in your heart toward God. The Lord has put a goal before you and that is maturity.

This is why Paul said in Hebrews 6:1, *"Therefore leaving the principles of the doctrine of Christ,* ***let us go on*** *unto perfection; not laying again the foundation of repentance from dead works, and of faith toward God."* Remember that getting saved is just the beginning. It is just the first step. God expects you to grow. This is why you are encouraged to go to Church, read the Bible, and be with other Christians. If you do these things you will grow strong and develop in God. Our God is an awesome God who is very real and does miracles.

Therefore, believe that He is committed to helping you overcome in all your areas of struggle.

In Summary:

- Do not be a secret Christian. Tell others about Jesus.
- Purpose to be strong and mature in Christ Jesus.
- Commit all your struggles and conflicts to the Lord.
- Go to Church and fellowship with other Christians.
- Love the Word of God and read it daily.
- Turn continually from all your sinful ways.
- Believe God to answer your prayers.

Recommended Reading for Further Study:

Changed from Glory to Glory – Repentance
by Robert Tucker
Zion Christian Publishers

Chapter Two

GROWING IN CHRIST

THE NEED TO BE A GROWING CHRISTIAN

Even as parents want their children to grow and develop physically, so God wants His children to grow. Yet the sad thing is that some people are Christians for a long time and still do not grow. Satan will do all he can to stop a person from living in victory, for his desire is that Christians would backslide and give up. Therefore, the Christian life cannot be thought of as just a blessed and easy life. There will be trials, difficulties, and tests but the Lord is with you to help you. You will have many victories, but there will be many battles as well. However, through the good and the bad God expects you to keep on growing, changing, and progressing.

When I was in India, sometimes I would see a dwarf – a man perhaps in his fifties who had a mature man's head, but a body the size of a small boy. My heart would be so saddened because he had not fully grown. Many Christians are just like that dwarf – they have been saved for many years, but never grow to full maturity.

God's heart is so very sorrowful when His children do not grow and mature in their Christian life. There are certain things that God expects you to do, if you desire to grow and please Him. He will give you the grace; however, you must do your part. God has not created robots—you have been given the choice to accept Christ or reject Him. Every day is a choice for you. Are you going to serve God or go back into the world?

If you have genuinely determined within your heart to serve God, there are two choices that lie before you. Are you going to be like the stunted dwarf that never grew, or are you going to go on to maturity in your Christian life? If you choose God's way, you can gain victory over the devil and the powers of darkness and you will be privileged to see God's miracles.

1.) FIRST KEY TO VICTORY—A KNOWLEDGE OF GOD'S WORD

In this chapter we are going to look at two distinct requirements for victory in Christ. The first key to victory is having knowledge of the Word of God. No matter who you are or how young or old you are, you must seek to understand and know God through His Word. This does not mean that you must be a learned scholar overnight. However, God expects you to start with the basic truths of His Word. 1 Peter 2:2: *"As newborn babes, desire the sincere milk of the word, that ye may grow thereby."*

So how is that newborn like a new Christian? When a mother gives birth to a child she must feed him in order to keep him alive and help him grow. How often is the baby fed? Every day! What is he fed? Milk. The mother does not immediately feed her newborn baby a T-bone steak. She starts by giving him milk, then bread, and later meat is introduced into his diet.

It is the same with us when we become newborn Christians. There is a progression in the spiritual realm as well as the natural. When we are first born again, God requires us to drink the milk of His Word so that we may grow. However, He also expects us to progress from there because He wants our knowledge of His Word to become a deeper and deeper reality within us.

Paul, writing in Hebrews 5:12-14, makes this truth abundantly clear when he says: *"For when for the time ye ought to be teachers, ye have need that one teach you again which be the first principles of the oracles of God; and are become such as have need of milk, and not of strong meat. For every one that useth milk is unskilful in the word of righteousness: for he is a babe. But strong meat belongeth to them that are of full age, even those who by reason of use have their senses exercised to discern both good and evil."*

Therefore if you desire to grow properly, you need to be in the Scriptures daily. We cannot say this enough! The Bible is God's voice—God speaking to us. It is, in fact, a revelation from God to man. Through His Word, God has given to all of mankind a special, infallible, supernatural revelation. God has spoken, and the Bible is the result of it. It is God's eternal Word. In Matthew 24:35, Jesus said, *"Heaven and earth shall pass away, but My words shall not pass away."* Psalm 138:2 also tells us that God puts His Word above His name, which further shows us how important it is for us to study and learn these precious truths.

The Beginnings of the Bible

The inspiration behind the Scriptures comes from the Holy Spirit. The Apostle Peter declares that *"...holy men of God spoke as they were moved (inspired) by the Holy Spirit"* (2 Pet. 1:21, NKJV). According to 2 Timothy 3:16, *"All scripture is given by inspiration of God."* The word "inspiration" actually means "God-breathed." All Scripture, every single word, is God-breathed. Therefore, our Bible is the product of the divine breath or Holy Spirit of God. It is the Holy Spirit speaking through men to man. It is the work of God (through the Spirit) in men, enabling them to receive and give us divine truths without error. The Holy Spirit so guided and controlled the men who wrote the Bible in the original languages, that what they wrote was exactly what God wanted to communicate.

The Bible is written by 44 different writers. Some of these men were kings, some were lowly fishermen, some were statesmen, one was a doctor, and one a tax collector. In an approximate span of 2,000 years, the Bible writers gave us the entire canon of Scripture, which is 66 books. Moses wrote the book of Genesis in approximately 1,500 B.C.; the book of Job was written before that; the last book, Revelation, was written in A.D. 96. Even though there were many writers over such a long span of years, God's Word was preserved throughout all the centuries of man. What a wonderful miracle! His Word is our way of life because He is alive. There is an explosive power in this book because Jesus is the living Word of God, who is revealed as the Christ to us through His book. It is a book that will change your life forever. Praise the Lord!

Bible Divisions

The Bible is divided into two Testaments, the Old and the New. Testament simply means "covenant." A covenant, or testament, only comes into being when someone dies. Hebrews 9:16-17 explains this fully: *"For where a testament is, there must also of necessity be the death of the **testator**. For a testament is of force after men are dead: otherwise it is of no strength at all while the **testator** liveth."*

So we see that both the Old and New Testaments required death, or the shedding of blood. In the Old Testament God required the shedding of the blood of animals, but this looked ahead to the New Covenant where God through His Son shed His own blood. Jesus Christ is the Testator of the New Testament. When

He died, all that He had promised as the Testator was accomplished. The blood of animals could not take away our sins or guilt, nor could it give us forgiveness. Only the sacrifice of Jesus upon the cross could remove our guilty stain of sin, for without the shedding of blood there is no forgiveness or eternal life for mankind. We have life only because Jesus died upon the cross and shed His blood as the perfect Sacrifice.

There are various divisions in the Bible that you should be aware of as you begin to study God's Word. The Old Testament is comprised of 39 books, which are divided as follows:

- **The Pentateuch** – Genesis through Deuteronomy (5)
- **The Historical Books** – Joshua through Esther (12)
- **The Poetical Books** – Job through Song of Solomon (5)
- **The Major Prophets** – Isaiah through Daniel (5)
- **The Minor Prophets** – Hosea through Malachi (12)

The Old Testament laid a solid foundation for the New Testament; the entire New Testament grew out of the Old. The New Testament begins with the four Gospels giving four accounts of the life of Christ, who lived for approximately 33 ½ years. It also deals with the first century Church. There are 27 books, which can be divided as follows:

- **Manifestation** – the Four Gospels (4)
- **Propagation** – the Book of Acts (1)
- **Explanation** – the Epistles: Paul's – 14, General – 7, (21 total)
- **Consummation** – the Revelation (1)

The first book of the Bible is Genesis, which is known as "the book of beginnings" because virtually every major truth has its origin in Genesis. The next books are Exodus, Leviticus, Numbers, and Deuteronomy. These four books cover the period from Israel's deliverance from Egyptian bondage to the end of their forty years in the wilderness. In Exodus, God gave Moses the Ten Commandments and the pattern for the Tabernacle. In Leviticus various feasts and offerings and ceremonial laws were instituted for the priests. Numbers brings us to the end of the forty years of wilderness journey. Deuteronomy is the second reading of the Law, given unto the new generation who had not heard it at Sinai 40 years earlier. Deuteronomy is composed also of various sermons and exhortations given by Moses at the end of his life, just before the new generation crossed over Jordan into the land of promise.

The Book of Joshua actually brings the new generation into the land of inheritance where they had to drive out their enemies. Judges and Ruth deal with the period after they had settled into the land of inheritance in which there were numerous backslidings among the people. Each time the people turned from God unto idolatry the Lord raised up enemies to vex His people in order to bring them to their senses. However, when the people turned back to God, He sent them judges (or deliverers) to set them free. The period of Judges lasted about 350 years.

Then we have Samuel, who anointed the first king, Saul. This inaugurated the reign of the kings and ended the era of the rule of judges. The books of I-II Samuel deal with this period. After Samuel anointed David, Israel's second king, there came that special period when many of the Poetical books were written, such as Psalms, Proverbs, and Ecclesiastes. Job was written much earlier but it is placed among the Poetical books.

The Psalms are a wonderful study that will tremendously help your devotional life as you spend time with the Lord. Proverbs has many pearls of wisdom that will teach you how to relate to people, how to keep yourself pure, and how to overcome anger, lust, vanity, etc. There are 31 chapters in Proverbs, and we encourage you to get into the habit of reading one chapter a day. This way you can read through it every month.

The reign of the kings lasted nearly 500 years, all the way up to the Babylonian captivity in 586 B.C. The books of I-II Kings and I-II Chronicles cover this period. During the reign of kings, most of the writing prophets had their ministry. This would include the four major prophets and most of the minor prophets. After the Babylonian captivity came the restoration period. The books of Ezra, Nehemiah, Esther, Haggai, Zechariah, and Malachi cover this period.

There is such a consistency in the Old and the New Testaments. All the New Testament writers uphold the authority of the Old Testament. The four Gospel writers—Matthew, Mark, Luke, and John—not only recorded the quotations of Jesus from the Old Testament, they also made similar quotations from, and allusions to the Old Testament. The Gospel writers all focused on the life of Jesus. Matthew, who is writing to the Jews, speaks of Jesus as King. Mark is written to the Romans and presents a Gospel of action that portrays Jesus as the ox, or the suffering Servant. Luke presents Jesus as the Son of Man who came to save the lost. Christ's humanity was a total identification with us. He was hungry and thirsty, and was tempted. He also wept and suffered from exhaustion. John's Gospel reveals Christ as the Son of God.

The Book of Acts has more than forty quotations and references from the Old Testament. The book of Acts records the sermons of Peter, Stephen, and Paul. It deals with the history of the early Church and how the Holy Spirit came; it gives us accounts of healing and miracles, as God manifested His mighty power. It is also a foretaste of what God wants to do today!

Then there are Paul's Epistles. Before his conversion, Paul hated Christianity, persecuting and killing many Christians until God confronted him on the Damascus Road. Paul was completely changed when he met the Lord. He became a mighty man of God who preached salvation through Christ to the Gentiles. The Book of Acts and Paul's epistles together reveal much of the Apostle Paul's missionary journeys, where many miracles were performed.

We also have the seven general epistles, which include James, 1,2 Peter, 1,2,3 John, and Jude. James and Jude, who were brothers of Jesus, were both unbelieving during the life and ministry of their Elder Brother, but both had a tremendous conversion after Christ's resurrection. As young men they were double-minded and unstable in all their ways. The Apostle Peter was the one who denied the Lord, but after the Holy Spirit came upon him he was filled with extraordinary boldness and led many to salvation. The Apostle John who was termed "ignorant and unlearned" by the clergy of his day, wrote the Book of Revelation.

Revelation focuses mainly upon the last three-and-a-half years of the Church Age where God separates the children of God from the children of the Devil. The Lord does this by allowing an imposter to come just before Christ. In so doing, all those who are not genuine are drawn away by the Antichrist.

From Genesis to Revelation, God has given us extensive evidence that His power is undeniable and indisputable. In the book entitled "God's Awesome Book" (which has genealogies, facts, history, and the hidden codes in the Bible), there are many proofs that verify that the Bible is the inspired Word of God. Many ancient people have stories and records of a flood that once covered the world. In Scripture there are about 300 prophecies concerning Christ's first coming and every one was fulfilled. There are eight times as many prophecies about the Second Coming of Christ as there were about His first coming; surely these also will be fulfilled.

It was prophesied in Micah 5:2 that out of Bethlehem a ruler would come forth and govern Israel. Zechariah prophesied that He would come riding into Jerusalem on a donkey (Zech. 9:9). Zechariah, who lived about 500 years before Christ, said prophetically that Christ would be sold for thirty pieces of silver. Scripture shows us that Judas sold Jesus for thirty pieces of silver (Zech. 11:13). Psalms 22:16 says, *"They pierced my hands and my feet."* Psalms 22:18 foretold *"They shall divide my clothes amongst them and throw dice for my garments"* (NKJV).

The chances of just eight Bible prophecies concerning the first coming of Christ being fulfilled are astronomical—not just one chance in a billion or a trillion but one chance in many, many trillion. In other words, take all the sand on all the seashores of the world and put that sand in just one country. Then take one grain of sand, color it purple, blindfold someone, and ask them to pick up that purple grain of sand—the chance of their choosing that grain of sand would not be as great as just eight prophecies being fulfilled. Yet actually, there were 300 prophecies fulfilled concerning Christ's first coming. Therefore, you and I can never underestimate the power of the Word of God to change and transform our lives.

God's Word Gives Victory over Sin

The Word of God used wisely can break the power of sin in your life. It is therefore your necessary food. You must hide it in your heart continually, and meditate upon it in order to grow in your Christian life. God's Word is your defense against your greatest enemies—the world, the flesh, and the devil. Scripture speaks clearly of the two natures within you that produce a warfare of heart, mind, and flesh.

Romans 8:1 is a great encouragement when it says: *"There is therefore now no condemnation to them which are in Christ Jesus, who walk not after the flesh, but after the Spirit."* Consequently, you will experience no condemnation only when you walk according to the Spirit and not according to the flesh. Sin causes you to rebel against God; but His Word changes your course, draws you unto Him, and convinces you to follow Him with your whole heart.

Psalm 119

We find in this precious Psalm that the major theme is the Word of God. Therefore, as a new believer, many verses in this particular Psalm should become very important to you. As you meditate upon it and study it, you will discover many keys that will enable you to overcome in the area of sin. You will also see the wonderful things that God's Word can accomplish in your life.

Some of the benefits you will receive are as follows:

1.) HIDING GOD'S WORD IN YOUR HEART HELPS YOU NOT TO SIN: The Psalmist said, *"Thy word have I* *hid in mine heart, that I might not sin against thee"* (v. 11). Like the Psalmist, you must be afraid to sin and take much care to prevent it. As you hide God's Word in your heart, it will help you to have victory over sin. You will increasingly be able to overcome temptation with the Word of God as Jesus did when He said, "It is written…!"

As you read and study God's Word, there will be times when a scripture will catch your attention and come alive to you. This is the time to meditate on it, and memorize it. God's Word will keep you from sin, or sin will keep you from God's Word.

2.) GOD'S WORD IS A STABLE FOUNDATION: With changing times and all the instability that is in the world today, the Word of God stands firm. It is a stable, solid, and established foundation that you can depend upon daily and even moment by moment as you walk out your new Christian life. *"For ever, O LORD, thy word is settled in heaven"* (v. 89).

3.) GOD'S WORD WILL GUIDE YOUR LIFE: *"Thy Word is a lamp unto my feet and a light unto my path"* (v. 105). This is the nature of the Word of God—it is a lamp and a light to guide you through life.

In some parts of Africa, snakes are often on overgrown paths. While walking at night, the Africans often tie a small lamp to their leg to see where to put their feet to avoid the snakes. They would also shine a flashlight on the path ahead to guide them and show them where to go. Like the lamp, God's Word will preserve you from dangers and traps of the enemy; like the light, it will guide you in all the decisions of life.

The Word of God gives guidance in many areas of life. For example, in the area of marriage, the Bible commands you not to be unequally yoked with unbelievers (2 Cor. 6:14). In other words, if you are a Christian, it is wrong to marry an unbeliever. The most important thing in life is to know Jesus. Therefore, if you are not married, your prayer should be that your life partner would be someone who has the same purpose and vision as you do. This way, you can share together, go to church together, and grow together in God.

4.) GOD'S WORD ENABLES YOU TO ENDURE AFFLICTION: *"I am afflicted very much; Revive me, O LORD, according to Your word"* (v. 107, NKJV). God's Word enables you to endure times of testing, trials, and difficulties that will surely come upon you. Yet during these times of difficulty, the Word will become very precious to you. In your Christian life, you will have times of discouragement, fears, and confusion. However, like the Psalmist, you can cry out for God's grace to revive you. During the difficult times, you too can stand on the promises of God and put your trust in them.

5.) GOD'S WORD IS A DELIGHT TO OUR TASTE: The Word of God is joyous. It is exciting. It speaks directly to you. Verse 103 says, *"How sweet are thy words unto my taste! yea,* ***sweeter than honey*** *to my mouth!"* There is such a wonderful pleasure and delight in the Word of God. This Scripture speaks to us of a spiritual taste, or an inward satisfaction of divine things that can only be gained through personal experience. The Psalmist tells us that for him the Word of God was so sweet, and no other pleasure was comparable to it. This is how it should also be with us. This is the unspeakable profit and advantage that can be gained by the Word of God.

6.) THE WORD OF GOD IS MORE PRECIOUS THAN GOLD: *"The law of thy mouth is better unto me than thousands of gold and silver"* (v. 72). God's Word should be better to you than gold, which is perishable. You should never set you heart upon earthly riches (which cannot satisfy and will pass away), but rather on the Word of God which will endure forever.

7.) THE WORD OF GOD BRINGS MUCH PLEASURE: *"****I rejoice at thy word,*** *As one who finds great treasure. I hate and abhor lying, But I love Your law"* (v. 162-163, NKJV). This verse should encourage you to take great pleasure in the Word of God, as you read, hear, and meditate upon it. The more reverence you have for the Word of God, the more joy you will find in it. It is, however, through opposition and trials that you come to rejoice in God's Word as you follow on to know the Lord in a greater way.

8.) THE WORD BRINGS MUCH PEACE: The Word brings much peace to those who love God. *"**Great peace have they** which love thy law: and nothing shall offend them"* (v. 165). As you get to know the Word of God more, you will come to a place of peace, where you have a new joy and satisfaction that you never before thought possible.

You may be in great trouble and sorrow from without, and yet you will be able to enjoy great peace from within. If you will love God's Word, you will have great peace and security. Nothing shall offend you, and nothing shall be a stumbling block to you to entangle you either in guilt or grief. Therefore, may God grant His manifold grace to you and bring you His peace.

9.) THE WORD OF GOD PROMOTES PRAISE: The Word will motivate you to praise God with all your heart and with all your being. *"Seven times a day do I praise thee, because of thy righteous judgments"* (v. 164). This Scripture makes it very clear that we are not only to praise God every day, but we are to praise Him often throughout the day. Praising God is a duty, but a joyous one. You should praise God in all situations.

Getting Started in the Word

The Holy Spirit has been sent to help you understand God's Word, but it is also important to have a plan as you read it. For example, rather than starting to read in Genesis which is the beginning of the Bible, we recommend that you begin in the New Testament with the Gospel of John. This profound Gospel reveals Christ, the Son of the living God. Among other important subjects in the book of John, there is an emphasis on "believing" which is so important to you as a new believer. *"But these are written, that ye might believe that Jesus is the Christ, the Son of God; and that believing ye might have life through his name"* (John 20:31). The Book of John will help to confirm your faith in Christ as the eternal Son of God, the true Messiah and Savior of the world.

You should read at least one chapter of John a day. We suggest that after finishing John's Gospel that you go to Matthew's Gospel and work your way consecutively through the New Testament all the way to the book of Revelation. Then you can begin reading through the Old Testament, starting in Genesis.

2.) A SECOND IMPORTANT KEY— PRAYER

The second key to your growth as a Christian is to learn the importance of prayer. In any relationship there must be communication if the relationship is to grow. My wife must talk to me and I to her if we desire to maintain a growing and lasting relationship. It is the same with you and God. God is a person. He is real. His desire is to have a close relationship with you. Therefore, communication through prayer is vital to your growth as a new believer.

Prayer is speaking to God; it is not complicated. The way you learn to pray is by practice. For example, if you want to learn to drive a car, you can read books, go to seminars, and learn all about the parts of a car, but you will still not be able to drive. You learn to drive by getting into the car and starting to drive. In the same way, we learn to pray by praying.

Some people think that prayer is just an empty religious ritual, but prayer is a personal intimacy with the living God. He loves you and He wants you to talk to Him. He also wants to answer your prayers. His desire is to be real and vital in your life. The Christian life is a life lived in close relationship with God, and for any relationship to be meaningful there must be a two-way conversation.

God speaks to you in many ways, but the principal way is through His Word. You in turn must speak to Him through prayer. The Word of God instructs you to pray continually. However, some people only feel they should pray when they have a need or a problem. Still others think that prayer is all about me, me, and me! Bless my family, bless my son, my daughter, my wife, etc. While God is pleased to bless us and supply our needs, prayer is more than just asking for blessings.

Spend Time Alone with God

James 4:8 assures us that if we will draw near to God, He will also draw near to us. It is important to draw near to God every day, reserving a portion of your day just for Him alone, preferably early in the morning before the busyness of the day. Make a special time to pray and read God's Word, a specific time to withdraw from the pressures of life and just simply get alone with God. If you want to grow as a Christian, this is such an essential step in your progress toward a mature walk with God.

Five Aspects of Prayer

1.) Thanksgiving

As you begin to pray, you should begin by thanking God for what He has done for you. Psalm 100:4 tells us to *"**Enter into His gates with thanksgiving**, And into His courts with praise, be thankful to him, and bless his name."* There are so many things for which we can thank God. While so many others choose to complain, murmur, and criticize, you must remember to thank Him continually. With a heart full of thanksgiving, David writes in Psalm 103:2: *"Bless the Lord, O my soul, and forget not all his benefits."*

2.) Worship

When you worship God begin by praising Him for what He has done for you. For as you give thanks to God and praise Him for what He has done, it will lead you to worship Him because of who He is. Then as you worship God with songs of adoration, you will find yourself focusing not on your own needs but on the beauty and majesty of the Lord. It is so important to think about the glory of God and His goodness. It is vital for you to pour out your love and admiration to the Lord, showing Him that He is your best friend and the lover of your soul.

The Book of Psalms is a good book to help with your worship, for it will bring the attributes of God before you and inspire you to worship Him in a deeper way. We also encourage you to go to Church and worship with others who love the Lord. Also, get a good worship tape and sing at home. This is so important because worship will change you to be more like the Lord. Jesus said in John 4:23-24, *"But the hour cometh, and now is, when the true worshippers shall worship the Father in spirit and in truth: for the Father seeketh such to worship him. God is a Spirit: and they that worship him must worship him in spirit and in truth."*

3.) Confession

The closer you get to the Lord, the more you will become aware of the sin that God needs to deal with and cleanse from your life. As we have already said, you are not going to be perfect overnight so this cleansing process will be ongoing. However, when you fail, you need to confess it and ask God for forgiveness and then make it right before Him. Psalm 66:18 says, ***"If I regard iniquity in my heart,***

The Lord will not hear me." In other words, if you sin and do nothing about it (if you do not repent), then God will not hear your prayers. However, if you are aware of your sin and deal with it in the correct way, God will hear your prayers.

It is important that you keep short accounts with God, for as you confess your sins and ask forgiveness, you are cleansed by His blood (1 Jn. 1:9).

4.) Intercession

This word comes from a Latin word, which literally means "to go between" or to take the place of the person for whom you are praying. Intercession is praying on behalf of others as the Holy Spirit directs you. You should get into the habit of praying for others before you pray for yourself. Come before God often on behalf of others. Jesus is our example, for He stands continually before the Father on our behalf after having totally identified with our needs as the Son of Man. Hebrews 7:25 tells us that He ever lives to make intercession for us.

Some examples of real intercessors in the Bible would include Abraham, as he prayed for Lot and his family to be saved from destruction in Sodom. Moses also prayed on behalf of three million Israelites when God sought to destroy them because of their idolatry. God spared the lives of those that were being prayed for, all because of the intercessory prayers of Moses. In the same way, you too can be used of God to intercede for others and receive wonderful answers from God. There will be times when the Holy Spirit will lay a person or situation on your heart and you will find yourself interceding for these needs.

5.) Supplication

This basically means that you should pray for the things you need. In the Lord's prayer Jesus said, *"Give us this day our daily bread"* (Matt. 6:11). God wants to bless you and supply all that you need.

A most important thing to remember when you pray is to expect God to answer! However, to receive answers to prayer you must be sure you are praying according to His will. In 1 John 5:14 we read: *"And this is the confidence that we have in him, that, if we ask anything* ***according to his will****, he heareth us: And if we know that he hear us, whatsoever we ask, we know that we have the petitions that we desired of him."* As you read God's Word, more and more you will be able to discern the will of God and know what and how to pray.

It is also important for you to pray in faith. Mark 11:24 says, *"Therefore I say unto you, What things soever ye desire, when ye pray, believe that ye receive them, and ye shall have them."*

Faith comes as a result of a word from God (Rom. 10:17). Therefore, if you pray according to His revealed will you can pray in total faith, believing He will answer.

When I was just a young believer, I went on a mission trip to New Guinea where I became very ill. When I collapsed and went into a coma, the doctors said I had a very severe case of malaria that had infected my brain. They also told my friends that I only had a few hours to live. The team of young people I was working with at that time began to pray. God spoke and then raised me up from my sick bed, and to this day I have never had any trace of malaria. I have seen so many miracles and prayers answered by God. Jesus is real! He is alive. So be assured that He can answer your prayers and help you grow mightily as a new Christian.

In Summary:

- Because God expects us to be growing Christians, two essential keys to growth are:
  1.) A knowledge of God's Word
  2.) Learning the importance of prayer

- **Psalm 119 describes the benefits received from study of the Word of God:**
  1.) It makes it more difficult to sin.
  2.) It is a stable foundation.
  3.) It will guide your life.

4.) It will enable you to endure affliction.
5.) It is a delight to our taste.
6.) It is more precious than gold.
7.) It brings much pleasure.
8.) It brings much peace.
9.) It promotes praise.

- **The five aspects of prayer are:**
  1.) **Thanksgiving** – beginning prayer with giving thanks to God
  2.) **Worship** – adoring God for who He is, not just for what He does
  3.) **Confession** – keeping short accounts with God
  4.) **Intercession** – praying for the needs of others
  5.) **Supplication** – praying for your own requests and for guidance

Recommended Reading for Further Study:

Biblical Introduction
by Dr. Paul Caram
Zion Christian Publishers

Prayer
by Joseph Cilluffo
Zion Christian Publishers

Chapter Three

GROWING IN GRACE

THE IMPORTANCE OF GRACE

As a new believer, you must understand the importance of grace in your new life as a Christian. 2 Peter 3:18 tells you to *"Grow in the grace and knowledge of our Lord and Savior Jesus Christ."* This verse emphasizes the importance of not just staying where you are, but also being able to develop and mature in your Christian walk. God's grace is defined as "unmerited favor," yet it is so much more. Grace is also divine enablement from God to enable you to accomplish what God has called you to do. It is so important to ask God for grace in every situation we face.

COMMUNION

One way that you will grow in grace as a believer is to partake of the blessings of communion. In 1 Corinthians 10:16, the Apostle Paul said, *"The cup which we bless, is it not the communion of the blood of Christ? The bread which we break, is it not the communion of the body of Christ?"*

The sacred act of communion is important because when you partake of communion, you are actually professing to be in friendship and fellowship with the Lord Jesus Christ. His body was broken and His blood was shed to obtain the forgiveness of your sins and the favor of God.

The Lord's supper is a time of partaking of the bread and wine because of the sacrificed body and blood of our Lord. To eat and drink of these sacraments is in a very real sense to partake of the sacrifice, because we are those for whom the sacrifice was offered. To partake of the Lord's table means that you are actually professing yourself to be one who is in covenant with Him.

In the Old Testament we read how the children of Israel were slaves in Egypt for many years. Before God miraculously delivered Israel, He sent a succession of judgments against the Egyptians. One of those judgments was the slaying of every firstborn son of the Egyptians. To protect the Israelites, God instructed them to kill a lamb and apply the blood to the door posts and lintel of their homes. At midnight when the death angel passed over, their firstborn sons would not be harmed (Exodus 12).

This historical event was actually a sign that pointed towards the death of Jesus, the Lamb of God, and the shedding of His righteous blood. The bread is a symbol of the body of Jesus that was broken for us (1 Cor. 11:24-25). The wine (juice) that we drink is a symbol of the blood of Jesus that was shed. Jesus told them to take these emblems, the bread and the wine, and do this in remembrance of Him. In 1 Corinthians 10:21, communion is referred to as "the Lord's table," and in 1 Corinthians 11:20 it is called "the Lord's supper."

At the end of each of the Gospels, in speaking of the Lord's Supper, the Scriptures tell us that the actual communion service—the bread and the wine (juice) are substances that are used to represent the body and blood of Jesus. Leviticus 17:11 says: *"For the life of the flesh is in the blood, and I have given it to you upon the altar to make atonement for your souls; for it is the blood that makes atonement for the soul."* The point here is that blood represents the life of a person. Therefore, when you partake of communion you are remembering the life of Christ that was sacrificed for you. Communion is an act of true love and devotion, but it is so much more.

1.) Communion Is Fellowship

Communion is fellowship with God and also fellowship with other believers. As you partake of the Lord's Supper, it is an act of participation that brings a special sense of the Lord's presence into your heart. The Word of God promises that as you draw near to God, He will also draw near to you. Likewise, as you are obedient in participating in the Lord's Supper, you will also become more conscious of the presence of God in your life.

Communion is also at the center of a Church's fellowship. Barriers vanish when you come together with your brothers and sisters around the table of the Lord, for there is a spiritual communion in this kingdom ordinance. The Scripture in 1 Corinthians 10:17 shows us this truth when it says that we are one bread and one body as we all partake of the one Bread, which is Jesus Christ.

The symbolism of communion is twofold. Jesus broke the bread into pieces and gave a fragment of this bread to each disciple. By His example He was showing us what it means to be part of His body. Each piece, or fragment, was a part of one loaf, just as each member is a part of the one body of Christ. Therefore, we come into oneness through Jesus Christ, the Bread of Life. In communion, this loaf of bread becomes a symbol of the crucified Savior. In a very real sense, to partake of these emblems together with other believers is to have communion with Christ together. As we partake together, God gives us a special bond with other Christians no matter what factors of race, social standing, educational level, or culture, and through this bond there is a oneness in the Spirit.

Shortly after my wife and I were married, we were pastoring a small church in New Zealand. There were different kinds of people who came to the church. Among the people who attended was a surgeon from the local hospital, laborers, young and old, rich and poor, whites, and brown-skinned Maori people. Some wondered how such different kinds of people could come together to fellowship, but it is really not difficult to understand when you realize the truth of coming together in Jesus. Each of these people had something in common, and that was Jesus Christ.

2.) *Communion Is Giving Thanks*

Communion is also symbolic of thanksgiving. In many Churches communion is referred to as the Eucharist, which is a Greek word that means thanksgiving. Luke 22:17 tells us: *"And he took the cup, and* ***gave thanks****, and said, Take this and divide it among yourselves."* Jesus gave thanks for the wine (the juice).

When Jesus first instituted this ordinance, He used only one cup from which they all drank. In verse 19, we see also that He gave thanks for the bread. Therefore, as we partake of communion with a heart overflowing with thanksgiving to the Lord for what He has done for us on the cross, it should encourage us to present our lives as a fresh offering unto Him.

3.) *Communion Is Only for Christians*

People who are not Christians should not take communion. It is only for people who are born again. Even as a believer, each time you take communion you should examine your heart to make certain that there is no sin in your life that needs to be confessed and forgiven. Your heart should be prepared before God, as communion can either be a blessing or a curse. We should therefore always take communion in the proper way. Some people have even died prematurely because they have taken communion in an unworthy manner. For example, if a Christian is deliberately living in sin, partaking in communion could bring judgment upon him.

First Corinthians 11:27-30 says, *"Therefore whoever eats this bread or drinks this cup of the Lord in an unworthy manner will be guilty of the body and blood of the Lord. But* ***let a man examine himself****, and so let him eat of the bread and drink of the cup. For he who eats and drinks in an unworthy manner eats and drinks judgment to himself, not discerning the Lord's body. For this reason many are weak and sick among you, and many sleep (are dead)"* (NKJV). This is a very serious matter to God, because anyone who partakes unworthily is making a mockery of the Son, and of His body and blood that He offered up for us.

Communion is a past, present, and even future reality for all believers because:

- We look into the past and remember what Jesus did on the cross for us. We also remember that by His stripes we are healed.
- Communion is more than just symbolic, for as you participate in this sacred ordinance you should believe God for a fresh impartation of His Spirit into your heart.
- You need to believe as you continue to partake of communion that it will cause you to grow in Christ.

First Corinthians 11:26 says, *"For as often as ye eat this bread, and drink this cup, ye do shew the Lord's death till he come."* Here Paul says that we are to continue partaking of the Lord's supper until the Second Coming of Christ.

FELLOWSHIP WITH OTHER CHRISTIANS

As we have already mentioned, another important key to growing in grace is to spend time with the right people. You must fellowship with those of a strong faith. We are all familiar with the old saying, "Birds of a feather flock together." If you are choosing to be with people who are anti-God, who are cursing and using the Lord's name in vain and who are telling dirty jokes, it will bring you down. However, if you are with people who love Jesus, they will lift you up and encourage you. Your closest friends should be people who have Jesus as their Lord, because they are your brothers and sisters in Christ from whom you can learn so much. Proverbs 13:20 says, *"He who walks with wise men will be wise, But the companion of fools will be destroyed"* (NKJV). In 1 Corinthians 15:33 we read, *"Do not be misled, Bad company corrupts good character"* (NIV).

FINDING FELLOWSHIP IN CHURCH

Another important key to growing in grace and the knowledge of God is finding a church where you can have good fellowship with other believers of like precious faith. Christian fellowship is such an important aspect of your new life in Christ. However, in so much of the world today there is a "go it alone" attitude, which often carries over into the Church world as well. Many Christians feel very free to go here and there to church, never getting planted in one particular fellowship where they can be fed spiritually and be accountable to the church leadership. Watching church on television is not an acceptable substitute for finding a good church and becoming a part of it.

You may hear some people say that they do not need to go to church, that they can worship God all by themselves. However, God has not ordained the Christian's life to be this way. In order to grow, you need relationships with others of like precious faith. We are told in Hebrews 10:25 not to forsake the gathering together with other Christians: *"Not forsaking the assembling of yourselves together, as the manner of some is..."* The reason for this is because God has purposed that these relationships will do a work within us. He wants to shape and mold us into His image, and often He uses other people to accomplish His purposes within our stubborn, rebellious hearts. We need each other. It is that simple.

To illustrate this point, let us picture a hot campfire burning brightly. If you remove one red hot, burning log from that fire, what happens to it? It goes out and the larger fire is diminished and grows weaker. Yet if you throw an extra log on that same fire, it will grow stronger. It is the same with us as Christians. If you stop going to church and fellowshipping with other Christians, not only will your spiritual life become weaker, but the church will be affected as well. However as you attend church regularly, your spiritual fire will burn brightly and the church will be strengthened also. Therefore, it is very important to be a part of a local Church and become involved.

When you do find the church that you feel comfortable being a part of, it is so necessary to develop friendships within that church. It is difficult to get to know people when you are only looking at the back of their necks for an hour and a half during the service. It is good to attend small groups, Sunday school, or perhaps a weekly Bible Study. These activities will help you get to know others who also desire to grow in their Christian life.

SHARING YOUR FAITH WITH OTHERS

Another way that you can grow in the grace of the Lord is to share your faith with others. As we have previously said, if you want to grow you cannot be a secret Christian. Jesus said in Luke 19:10, *"For the Son of man is come to seek and to save that which was lost."* Jesus came to seek and save the lost, and He has given you the grace to also do the same. God wants to use you to reach people with the Gospel. In Mark 5:19, we read about a man who was possessed with many demons. After Jesus delivered him, the Lord told him to go home and tell his friends about the good things that God had done for him. Mark 16:15 instructs us to go into the entire world and preach the Gospel to every creature. In other words, we are to go and tell others the good news of Jesus Christ.

However, witnessing is not just what you say, but it is also how you live. You cannot tell someone how to be saved and how wonderful Jesus is and then go out and live like the Devil. To be convincing, your life must measure up to your message. The walk must match the talk. What you say must agree with how you live. Paul writes to the believers in Corinth in 2 Corinthians 3:2: *"Ye are our epistle written in our hearts, known and read of all men."* From this Scripture we see that God intends for your character and lifestyle to show forth Christ; therefore, it is not just by your words only that you are a witness for Christ. Jesus said in Matthew 5:16: *"Let your light so shine before men, that they may see your good works, and glorify your Father which is in heaven."*

Sharing the "Good News" of Jesus Christ or choosing to remain silent about your faith can be compared to the difference between the Sea of Galilee and the Dead Sea in Israel. The River Jordan flows into the Sea of Galilee and out again, and then goes downward into the Dead Sea. As a result of the river flowing in and out of the Sea of Galilee, this body of water is full of life and a variety of fish.

However, the Dead Sea has the River Jordan flowing into it but there is no outflow. Thus the water that comes in simply evaporates. The Dead Sea is so full of salt and minerals that nothing can live in this water. Therefore, it is just like its name—the Dead Sea. It is the lowest place on earth at 1300 feet below sea level.

We can compare this natural example to our spiritual life in Christ. When you come to church and you receive the Word of God, you are not just to keep it to yourself. As you learn to witness and give out to others, you will be fruitful and full of life like the Sea of Galilee. If you do not tell others about the Lord you will become like the Dead Sea. We must never be ashamed to share Christ with others. Jesus said, *"Whosoever therefore shall confess me before men, him will I confess also before my Father which is in heaven. But whosoever shall deny me before men, him will I also deny before my Father which is in heaven"* (Matt. 10:32-33).

Many people say, "I don't know the Bible very well. I don't know the answers." But you do know something that is very important. You know that once you were blind and were lost, but now, praise God, you are found and your eyes have been opened. You also know that Jesus died for your sins and you are forgiven. So go out and share what you know and how Jesus has changed your life. God's grace is with you; therefore, be encouraged. Be bold! Tell everyone about Jesus, for He is worthy!

In Summary:

- Understand the importance of communion and regularly partake of it, for it is a form of fellowship and thanksgiving to God.
- Develop good, healthy friendships with other godly people.
- Become regularly involved in a good Spirit-filled church where the Word of God is taught.
- Do not hide your faith, but share with others how the Lord has saved you and changed you.

Chapter Four

Baptism in Water

BAPTISM—AN ORDINANCE OF THE CHRISTIAN LIFE

When we consider the subject of baptism in water, there are different ideas or theories. Some churches do it one way and other churches do it another way. However, God's Word makes it very clear that there is only one way. Plainly Scripture tells us that water baptism is one of the ordinances of the Christian life. Therefore, as a born again believer who desires to move on with God, you must be water baptized. Otherwise, the foundation of your spiritual life will not be strong.

On the day of Pentecost, as Peter was preaching a powerful and anointed sermon, many cried out in conviction, *"What shall we do?"* Peter's answer to them in Acts 2:38 was, *"Repent, and be baptized every one of you in the name of Jesus Christ for the remission of sins, and ye shall receive the gift of the Holy Ghost."* We see here three very important steps which make a strong foundation for your Christian life. These are repentance, water baptism, and receiving, or being baptized in the Holy Spirit (which will be covered in chapter six).

JESUS WAS BAPTIZED BY IMMERSION

Christ's life shows you the pattern for your life. Jesus was baptized as a pattern for you to follow. It is also clear from Scripture that Jesus was not baptized as a baby. He was a full-grown adult. It is interesting to note that before Jesus did any miracles, before He preached any sermons, before he healed the sick and cast out demons, He came to the River Jordan and was baptized by John the Baptist.

In Matthew 3:13-15 we read, *"Then Jesus came from Galilee to John at the Jordan to be baptized by him. And John tried to prevent Him, saying, "I need to be baptized by You, and are You coming to me?" But Jesus answered and said to him, "Permit it to be so now, for thus it is fitting for us to fulfill all righteousness. Then he allowed Him"* (NKJV). Jesus knew that His obedience in being baptized was not only pleasing to His Father, it was the fulfillment of righteousness.

We see in the next verse that Jesus was fully immersed in water: *"And Jesus, when he was baptized, went up straightway out of the water"* (Matt. 3:16). If Jesus came up out of the water, then He must have first gone down into the water. Therefore, He was not just sprinkled, but fully immersed. At this moment, the heavens were opened and the Holy Spirit of God descended like a dove upon Him. The Father's voice from Heaven proclaimed, *"This is My beloved Son, in whom I am well pleased"* (Matt. 3:17).

The whole Godhead—Father, Son, and Holy Spirit—were there at the baptism of the Lord Jesus Christ. It was a very wonderful experience for Him. From this we see that Jesus was not only the Son of God by birth, He was now the Son of God by anointing when the Holy Spirit came upon Him in the form of a dove. The name Jesus means "Savior," and the name Christ means "the Anointed One." Jesus became the Anointed One after He fulfilled all righteousness by being baptized in water.

We have seen that at the beginning of His ministry, Jesus was baptized. Also, at the end of His ministry when Jesus gave the great commission, He spoke of the importance of being baptized. In Matthew 28:18-20 we read what Jesus said after His resurrection: *"And Jesus came and spoke to them, saying, "All authority has been given to Me in heaven and on earth. "Go therefore and make disciples of all the nations, baptizing them in the name of the Father and of the Son and of the Holy Spirit, "teaching them to observe all things that I have commanded you; and lo, I am with you always, even to the end of the age. Amen"* (NKJV). It is clear from this passage that water baptism is to be administered by the Church on the authority of Jesus Christ.

BAPTISM IN THE NEW TESTAMENT WAS BY IMMERSION

Water baptism as practiced in the New Testament was by full immersion. In Acts 8:35-38 we read, *"Then Philip opened his mouth, and began at the same scripture, and preached unto him Jesus. And as they went on their way, they came unto a certain water: and the eunuch said, See, here is water; what doth hinder me to be baptized? And Philip said, If thou believest with all thine heart, thou mayest. And he answered and said, I believe that Jesus Christ is the Son of God. And he commanded the chariot to stand still: and they went down both into the water, both Philip and the eunuch; and he baptized him."* Here again we see the same evidence of someone going down into the water when they are baptized.

John 3:23 records a time when John the Baptist was baptizing near Salim because there was much water there. Obviously, much water is not needed if baptism is a practice by which one is sprinkled. Furthermore, if we study the root meaning of the English word "baptism," it is a transliteration of the Greek word "baptizo." This Greek word means to make fully wet or to immerse, which means when baptizing we should not just pour a few drops of water upon the head of a person. This word does not mean to sprinkle, it means to dip or to plunge. In the classical Greek, this word was used to describe a ship that had sunk and was completely immersed in water both inside and outside.

It was also used to describe a garment that had been completely immersed in a liquid dye. If for example a woman had a white dress and wanted to change the color of the dress to red, she would immerse the dress in a vessel of red dye solution. After some time she would take out the dress that was now changed to a red color, declaring that her dress had been baptized.

There are various ideas on the methods of baptism. Some believe that babies should be baptized, and still others believe that if you are not baptized you will not go to Heaven. However, neither of these are Scriptural. The thief on the cross was not baptized, but Jesus said to him when he asked to be remembered by Him, *"Today you will be with me in Paradise"* (Luke 23:43, NKJV).

You are saved and ready for Heaven when you repent of your sins and believe in Jesus. You are saved by faith through what Jesus has done. Salvation is not by works, nor does it depend upon being a good person, giving to charitable organizations, living a good life, or even going to church. While all these things are good, they cannot earn your salvation. The blood of Christ alone saves you. Yet if you are going to grow and go on with the Lord, water baptism is a very important step.

Because of the difference of opinion on this issue of water baptism, questions often arise. Part of the reason for this dates back to the 17th century, 1611, when the King James Version of the Bible was translated into English. At this time, there were many translations that came from many theologians who could not agree on the true meaning of baptism. Therefore, they did not translate the original Greek word "baptism" correctly into English. As we have already said, the actual definition of the Greek word "baptiso" is "to immerse."

Because of the confusion that has so often surrounded this subject, perhaps you too, as a new believer may have questions regarding what to do. If you have only been sprinkled, you need to be baptized by immersion. Suppose you have been previously baptized by immersion, but you now realize that you were only doing what others were doing and were not truly born again at the time. Then you should be baptized again because your heart was not changed before you went into the water. Many people also question whether a person who has received Christ and was baptized should be rebaptized if they fall away from the Lord for a season. Generally speaking, this is not advisable, because we do not find a Scriptural basis for it. There is nothing in the Word of God that requires or even suggests that being rebaptized is necessary, if you were genuinely saved when you were first baptized.

WHO QUALIFIES FOR BAPTISM?

- **Those who receive the Word of God.**

In Acts 2:41 we read, *"Then they that gladly received his word were baptized: and the same day there were added unto them about three thousand souls."* In this case, three thousand people gladly received the Word of God, firmly believed in Christ, and made an open profession of their faith in Him.

• Those who repent from their sins.

In verse 38 of this same passage, Peter said to them, *"Repent and be baptized every one of you in the name of Jesus Christ."* To repent means to have a change of mind or to turn and go in the opposite direction. Repentance means confessing our sins to the Lord, being sorry for them, and being willing to forsake them. Proverbs 28:13 says, *"He who covers his sins will not prosper, but whoever confesses and forsakes them will have mercy"* (NKJV).

• Those who believe and have faith in Jesus.

In Acts 2:38, it tells us that they had to be baptized in the name of Jesus Christ. Why did he stress this to the Jews? Because the Jews already did believe in the Father and the Holy Spirit, who they knew spoke to them through the prophets; but they did not yet believe or know Jesus as their Savior. Peter was making it clear to them that they must also believe in Jesus, the Christ and the promised Messiah.

When Philip was explaining about Jesus from the Old Testament to the Ethiopian eunuch, the eunuch asked, "What hinders me from being baptized?" In Acts 8:37-38, Philip answered, *"Then Philip said, "If you believe with all your heart, you may." And he answered and said, "I believe that Jesus Christ is the Son of God."...And both Philip and the eunuch went down into the water, and he baptized him"* (NKJV).

WHEN SHOULD YOU BE BAPTIZED?

Most accounts in the book of Acts indicate that baptism came immediately after repentance and believing in Christ. We see an example of this in Acts 16:30-33: *"And he brought them out and said, "Sirs, what must I do to be saved?" So they said, "Believe on the Lord Jesus Christ, and you will be saved, you and your household."* Then they spoke the word of the Lord to him and to all who were in his house. *"And he took them the same hour of the night and washed their stripes. And immediately he and all his family were baptized."* The point here is that the jailer and his entire household were baptized immediately, even though it was the middle of the night.

Therefore, it is best to be baptized as soon as possible after getting saved. As Psalm 119:60 says, *"I made haste, and delayed not to keep thy commandments."* In other words, if you have received the free gift of God's grace through salvation, you should not put off obeying the Lord's command to be baptized.

BONDAGES ARE BROKEN THROUGH BAPTISM

Something good happens when we are baptized. Through baptism, we have seen many bondages broken and people marvelously set free. When my wife and I were first married, we pioneered a church in the north of New Zealand. At first it was very difficult, but after about a year God gave us a breakthrough when a number of people were wonderfully saved. Some of these were involved in drugs, immorality, and false religions which had brought many bondages in their lives. After they received the Lord, one young man who had been involved in drugs and the occult was not only baptized in water, but was also baptized in the Holy Spirit at the same time. He was set free and continued to grow strong in the Lord. Later he became a pastor and missionary, bringing hundreds of people to the Lord.

Another young man that was saved was a surfer whom we picked up in our car when he was hitchhiking. We talked to him about the Lord, and invited him to church. He came the next Sunday and accepted Jesus as his Savior. A week later we baptized him, and as a result he was so changed that he stopped doing drugs and broke up with the girl he had been living with. After some time, he went to Bible School, and actually became the pastor of the church some years later. These examples show us that there is victory and freedom associated with the act of water baptism.

BAPTISM IDENTIFIES YOU WITH CHRIST'S DEATH, BURIAL, AND RESURRECTION

When you are baptized, you are expressing your faith in Jesus Christ. It is an outward, public expression of something that has taken place in your heart. You are publicly saying that you have committed your life to Christ and want to live for Him.

When you are baptized, you are identifying with the death, burial, and resurrection of Jesus. Romans 6:3-5 tells us: *"Know ye not, that so many of us as were baptized into Jesus Christ were baptized into his death? Therefore we are buried with him by baptism into death: that like as Christ was raised up from the dead by the glory of the Father, even so we also should walk in newness of life. For if we have been planted together in the likeness of his death, we shall be also in the likeness of his resurrection."*

After Jesus died on the cross, His body was buried in the grave. Three days later, He was gloriously raised from the dead. Your old sinful nature was crucified with Christ on the cross. What do you do when someone dies? You bury him. As you go into the waters of baptism, you are being buried with Christ. As Christ rose from the dead, so you come up out of the water to walk with Him in newness of life.

BAPTISM IS A STEP OF OBEDIENCE

Baptism by immersion is a step of obedience towards God. Jesus said in John 14:15, *"If you love me, keep my commandments."* If someone tells you he loves Jesus, but will not be baptized, it is questionable whether he truly loves Him. The Word of God commands you to "repent and be baptized" (Acts 2:38), so if you love Him, you will want to obey His Word and be baptized.

My wife and I lived in India for thirteen years. In the Hindu and Muslim mind, a person becomes a Christian when he is baptized in water. For many of them there is a tremendous cost involved when they obey the Lord and are baptized. They face much opposition and persecution from their own family members. In some cases, they are disowned by their families and even killed!

One Indian pastor shared the following testimony with me. As a young man, he and his wife were living in his father's house. After he accepted Jesus as His Savior, he read in the Scriptures about the need to be baptized in water. He decided to obey the Lord and get baptized. His father became very angry and shouted at him, "If you get baptized, you are not my son, and I am not your father. You will lose all of your inheritance."

Yet this faithful young man still chose to put his love for God first and was baptized in the river near his home. As a result, his father made him leave the house. Even his wife left him for a period of time. He suffered greatly with many hardships, but later his wife returned to him, and he went on to start many churches in India. Many years later when he talked with me, there were 68 members of his family and relatives that had since accepted the Lord, been baptized in water, and filled with the Holy Spirit. He had paid a great price, but he also saw God do many wonderful miracles.

OLD TESTAMENT SYMBOLS OF WATER BAPTISM

There are a number of spiritual types or symbols of water baptism in the Old Testament. For example, in Noah's time, God baptized (by the flood) the entire world in water to destroy all ungodly flesh so that a new order of life might begin. However, Noah and his family of eight emerged from the waters of this flood to walk in newness of life. Therefore, the same water that judged all flesh also preserved believing Noah and his family (Genesis chapters 6-8). In 1 Peter 3:20-21, Peter speaks of Noah's flood as a type of water baptism: *"Which sometime were disobedient, when once the longsuffering of God waited in the days of Noah, while the ark was a preparing, wherein few, that is, eight souls were saved by water. The like figure whereunto even baptism doth also now save us (not the putting away of the filth of the flesh, but the answer of a good conscience toward God,) by the resurrection of Jesus Christ."*

In the journey of the children of Israel, they first came out of Egypt, which is a type of the world. This is a picture of being saved out of the world by the blood of the Lamb (Exodus chapter 12). They then came to the Red Sea, which God miraculously parted and they went through on dry ground. The waters then returned and buried the Egyptians and their chariots. The crossing of the Red Sea symbolizes water baptism. In 1 Corinthians 10:1-2 we read: *"Moreover, brethren, I would not that ye should be ignorant, how that all our fathers were under the cloud, and all passed through the sea; And were all baptized unto Moses in the cloud and in the sea."*

After we are saved, the next major step in our Christian life is to be baptized in water. The Red Sea separated the children of Israel from Egypt, and water baptism speaks of a separation from this world. Just as the Red Sea delivered them from the bondage of their taskmasters, so water baptism breaks many bondages in our lives. At the Red Sea, Pharaoh's power over the Israelites was broken, and at water baptism there is a breaking of Satan's power over our lives as well. The Red Sea also destroyed their enemies who were trying to take them back to Egypt. In the same way, water baptism breaks the influence of those who seek to bring us back into the world. Thus, from this Old Testament type, we see the power of water baptism.

WHAT ABOUT YOU?

In view of the teaching in this chapter from God's Word, as a new born-again believer, we strongly encourage you to be baptized by immersion if you have not already done so. For through this step of obedience, you will move forward in God's wonderful purposes for your life.

In Summary:

- Baptism means *immersion.* Believers must be immersed.
- Baptism by immersion is only for true born-again believers.
- Baptism should *soon* follow new birth, not years later.
- Baptism breaks many bondages.
- Baptism identifies us with Christ's death, burial, and resurrection.
- Baptism is an act of obedience.

Chapter Five

JESUS – YOUR DELIVERER

GOD DESIRES TO DELIVER HIS PEOPLE

Jesus is your Savior, but He is also your deliverer. He is the One who has saved you from your sins, but He also desires to set you completely free. Two thousand years ago, Jesus came working miracles—healing the sick, raising the dead, and casting out demons. During His earthly ministry of three-and-a-half years, He not only continually healed the sick, but He also went about everywhere casting out evil spirits and setting people free. Acts 10:38 tells us, *"How God anointed Jesus of Nazareth with the Holy Ghost and with power: who went about doing good,* ***and healing all that were oppressed of the devil;*** *for God was with him."* Since Scripture tells us that Jesus is the same yesterday, today, and forever, we see clearly that His desire is to deliver people from every bondage and oppression.

THE DELIVERANCE MINISTRY OF JESUS

Early in the earthly ministry of Jesus in Luke 4:18, we read, *"The Spirit of the Lord is upon me, because he hath anointed me to preach the gospel to the poor; he hath sent me to heal the brokenhearted, to preach deliverance to the captives, and recovering of sight to the blind, to set at liberty them that are bruised."*

This particular Scripture was a quote from the book of Isaiah, a prophet who had lived over seven hundred years before Jesus was born (Isa. 61:1). Here Jesus is telling us that He was sent to preach, to heal, and to proclaim liberty to the captives. In other words, He came to set us free in every way. This is such an important reality for all new Christians to understand, for God longs to change your life and set you free!

THE AUTHORITY OF JESUS

In Mark 1:21-27, when Jesus and His disciples went to Capernaum, we see Him on the Sabbath exercising His authority in the area of deliverance. *"Then they went into Capernaum, and immediately on the Sabbath He entered the synagogue and taught. And they were astonished at His teaching, for He taught them as one having authority, and not as the scribes. Now there was a man in their synagogue with an unclean spirit. And he cried out, saying, "Let us alone! What have we to do with You, Jesus of Nazareth? Did You come to destroy us? I know who You are—the Holy One of God!" But Jesus rebuked him, saying, "Be quiet, and come out of him!" And when the unclean spirit had convulsed him and cried out with a loud voice, he came out of him. Then they were all amazed, so that they questioned among themselves, saying, "What is this? What new doctrine is this?*

***For with authority He commands even the unclean spirits, and they obey Him*"** (NKJV).

This was a man who was in the synagogue, not just someone Jesus came upon out in the streets of the city. Scripture does not tell us, but he was probably a very ordinary man with a very ordinary way of life until He had a divine encounter with Jesus.

Upon seeing Jesus and recognizing the authority within Him, the distressed demon cried out in verse 24, *"Let* ***us*** *alone! What have* ***we*** *to do with You, Jesus of Nazareth? Did You come to destroy* ***us****?* ***I*** *know who You are..."* Thus we can conclude that it is the demon and not the man speaking. Also, since the spirit said *we* and *us*, it is obvious that there was more than one demon residing within this man. However, one demon was speaking for itself and on behalf of others. Likewise, the demon in the man of Gadara who was filled with demons used the same form of speech: *"****My*** *name is Legion, for* ***we*** *are many"* (Mark 5:9).

What then did Jesus do? *"But Jesus rebuked him, saying, "Be quiet, and come out of him!" And when the unclean spirit had convulsed him and cried out with a loud voice, he came out of him"* (v. 25-26). We see that there was a significant battle here between the evil spirits and God, which also obviously affected the man. However, Jesus did not deal with the man, He dealt with the demon. He spoke with authority to the demon, not to the man.

Sometimes, as in this case, the demonic spirit will come out with a loud voice. Demons may also come out with a scream or a roar; they may even try to cause damage to the man or woman they are afflicting. At other times, a demon will simply come out quietly.

As you read through the Gospels you will discover numerous occasions when Jesus went about casting out demons. Some of these people were good, respectable people, but for whatever reason a demon had gained access to some part of their personality and as a result they were not in complete control. It is important to acknowledge the reality of demons, always remaining open to the truth that your life before you accepted Christ may have brought certain bondages.

Jesus also gave His disciples authority to cast out evil spirits and set the captives free. *"And he called unto him the twelve, and began to send them forth by two and two; and gave them power over unclean spirits"* (Mark 6:7). We also see in verse 13 of this same chapter that they were able through His authority to cast out many demons (see also Luke 9:1).

THE DELIVERANCE MINISTRY IN THE EARLY CHURCH

In the Book of Acts, we find that many people were delivered of evil spirits. For example, in Acts 8:6-7 we read about Philip: *"And the people with one accord gave heed unto those things which Philip spake, hearing and seeing the miracles which he did. For unclean spirits, crying with loud voice, came out of many that were possessed with them: and many taken with palsies, and that were lame, were healed."*

Another Scriptural example is when the Apostle Paul was ministering in Philippi. In this city was a woman who had the power to tell people's future by the spirit of divination. *"And it came to pass, as we went to prayer, a certain damsel possessed with a spirit of divination met us, which brought her masters much gain by soothsaying: The same followed Paul and us, and cried, saying, These men are the servants of the most high God, which shew unto us the way of salvation. And this did she many days. But Paul, being grieved, turned and said to the spirit, I command thee in the name of Jesus Christ to come out of her. And he came out the same hour. And when her masters saw that the hope of their gains was gone, they caught Paul and Silas, and drew them into the marketplace unto the rulers"* (Acts 16:16-19).

The Apostle Paul knew by revelation from God when to begin to deal with this spirit. After several days, he commanded the demon of divination to come out, and the woman was wonderfully delivered. However, since she was no longer able to predict the future of the townspeople, it caused quite an uproar in the city. This account therefore serves as a warning to us to rid ourselves of anything associated with fortune telling, such as horoscopes, tarot cards, palm reading, and any books or objects associated with witchcraft or the psychic realm: *"Many of them also which used curious arts brought their books together, and burned them before all men: and they counted the price of them, and found it fifty thousand pieces of silver"* (Acts 19:19).

GOD HAS GIVEN US AUTHORITY OVER DEMONS

Satan, who is called the prince of this world, was legally defeated when Jesus died on the cross and rose again. This defeat at Calvary dealt a deathblow to Satan and because of this we can have authority over him. Yet we must continually fight the good fight of faith and allow God to cleanse all our wrong motives, secret sins, bitterness, hatred, and all other bondages that would keep us from the freedom and liberty that God desires for our lives.

Satan binds many people, yet the Lord wants all His children to have a true and lasting victory. After we have been set free He wants to use us to help others to receive deliverance. Luke 10:19 shows us the power and authority that God has chosen to give to His people over evil spirits. *"Behold, **I give unto you power** to tread on serpents and scorpions, and over all the power of the enemy: and nothing shall by any means hurt you."* (Serpents and scorpions are a type of demons).

Forty days after the resurrection of Christ, He ascended up into heaven. Shortly before His ascension, He gave all believers a promise: *"And these signs shall follow them that believe; In my name shall they cast out devils"* (Mark 16:17). By these words, Jesus is actually giving you the authority and the power to have the victory over the devil and all his demons. Yet before you can drive out evil spirits in others, you must be absolutely certain that your own heart is cleansed and set free. Otherwise, you will have no authority over the enemy.

CAN CHRISTIANS HAVE A DEMON?

Often when we speak of deliverance, many people think of the demon-possessed man in Mark chapter 5 who could not even be held by chains because he was possessed with so many demons. As a missionary in India, I saw some people who were totally deranged and controlled by demon spirits. Some of the more severe cases I witnessed would walk around naked on the streets, totally out of their minds.

However, it is also a fact that many ordinary people are in bondage to Satan, although they are not possessed to this degree. Unfortunately, even many Christians who have accepted Christ as their Savior have areas in their lives that Satan still controls. In these cases, the word "possessed" is not the best word to use. Rather it can be clarified by saying that in one or more areas of their lives, instead of being under the control of the Holy Spirit, they are under the control of an evil spirit.

Let us give an illustration that will help explain this further. If you have a house with many rooms, and you have access to all of the rooms in the house except one that is locked up and full of garbage you would obviously not be in total control of your house. It is the same in many Christians' lives. Jesus may be the Lord of most areas in their lives, but one or two areas like those locked rooms can still be under the control of demons. To change you and deliver you, God needs to be in control of every area of your heart, soul, and mind.

As a new Christian, you may be progressing well in your walk with the Lord in many areas. However, there still may be areas where you are struggling and cannot get the victory because Satan still has control. For example, you may have deep-rooted fears, anger, lust, or jealousy, etc. Yet Jesus wants you to be free from all of these things. John 8:36 tells us, *"If the Son therefore shall make you free, ye shall be free indeed."*

There are some churches that teach that Christians cannot have a demon. Some also say that demons do not exist today, that these Scriptural examples were just concerning the time of the New Testament Church. But this is not an accurate assessment of the Scriptures, and the result of this kind of teaching leaves many people struggling for years in their bondages, never getting complete victory in their Christian lives. Demons do exist. They are very real, and you must be aware that areas of weakness in your life can be the result of having a demon or evil spirit.

We need to be careful not to take this ministry to the extreme as some people have done. Unfortunately, there are some who think that every difficulty a person has is the result of a demon. Consequently, they are always trying to cast out something. This is faulty reasoning, for many of the problems Christians encounter can be explained simply as *works of the flesh.*

Galatians 5:19-21 gives a list of these human failings: *"now the works of the flesh are evident, which are: adultery, fornication, uncleanness, lewdness, idolatry, sorcery, hatred, contentions, jealousies, outbursts of wrath, selfish ambitions, dissensions, heresies, envy, murders, drunkenness, revelries, and the like; of which I tell you beforehand, just as I also told you in time past, that those who practice such things will not inherit the kingdom of God"* (NKJV).

In other words, just because someone has an anger problem, this does not necessarily mean they have a spirit of anger. It can also be a work of the flesh – their old sinful nature. However, if they continually get so angry that there is no restraint they are opening themselves up for a spirit of anger to enter. Therefore, the remedy for our fleshly nature is crucifixion, but the only remedy for demons is to cast them out.

As a new believer it is important to understand that the solution to every problem is not deliverance. Yet on the other hand, the balance to this serious issue is that many Christians need to be freed from a particular bondage in their life. This is nothing to be ashamed of or concerned about, as most of the people who received assistance from Jesus during His earthly ministry were normal, respectable people.

THE CHARACTERISTICS OF DEMONS

Demons are believed to be the disembodied spirits of a former civilization. Therefore, because they used to live in bodies, they desire to inhabit a body. Demons have personalities just as we do. They have a mind and a will. They also have feelings and emotions. This is seen in the account of the demoniac of Gadara in Mark 5:2-13, who was sovereignly delivered from the evil spirits that had so long possessed him.

Matthew 8:29 also shows us that demons are conscious of coming judgment, for they cried out in the man, saying, *"Have You come here to torment us before the time?"* (NKJV). Demons know there is a set time for their judgment. Luke 8:31 records the demons begging Jesus not to send them into the *"deep"* (hell). Instead, they asked to be sent into a herd of pigs, preferring to inhabit the bodies of animals than to be disembodied. Jesus permitted them, but the pigs ran wildly off the cliff into the sea and were all drowned. Demons are looking for a home in which to dwell (see

Matthew 12:43-45) and will enter a heart that is open to them. Therefore, let us give no place to the devil, as Paul exhorts us in Ephesians 4:27 (see also Acts 5:3).

SOME SICKNESSES ARE CAUSED BY DEMONS

There are a number of reasons why people are sick, and sometimes sickness is caused by demons. In Matthew 9:32-33, Jesus healed a dumb man by casting out a dumb spirit. Jesus rebuked a fever because He knew in this case it was a demon that was causing the fever (Luke 4:38-39). We read in Luke 13:11, *"And, behold, there was a woman which had a spirit of infirmity eighteen years, and was bowed together, and could in no wise lift up herself."* This verse makes it clear that this was a spirit, not just a physical illness.

While I was in India, I had an experience I will never forget. I was speaking one night in a village in an open field. After preaching a simple salvation message, I gave an altar call asking people to repent and receive Christ as their Savior; several hundred responded. I then felt prompted of the Lord to call out all those who were deaf, and five people came forward. As I prayed for the first person, I put my hands over his ears and said, "In the name of Jesus, you deaf spirit, come out!" Immediately his ears were opened and he was able to hear. I prayed in the same way for the others and all were miraculously delivered and healed. In each of these cases, it was a spirit of deafness that was causing them not to be able to hear.

HOW DO EVIL SPIRITS GET INTO A PERSON?

There are various ways that demons gain access to human personalities.

- Scripture is very clear that we can inherit a generational iniquity such as idolatry, anger, jealousy, bitterness, lust, self-hatred, etc. Exodus 20:5 says, *"Thou shalt not bow down thyself to them, nor serve them: for I the LORD thy God am a jealous God, visiting the iniquity of the fathers upon the children unto the third and fourth generation of them that hate me."* (See also Ex. 34:7, Lev. 26:40, Num. 14:18, Deut. 5:9, 1 Sam. 3:13).

Even those inherent weaknesses in our parents (such as alcoholism, heart disease, diabetes, or various mental disorders) can be passed on and inherited by the children. For example, if a mother is into witchcraft or there has been a family background in the occult, often her child when he or she is born has this same iniquity, even though the child has not yet sinned in this area. We are very affected by the sins of our parents. Often if a father is an alcoholic, his son will also be an alcoholic. If a mother dies at 40 because of a heart condition, often she has a daughter who will have the same condition, which causes her death a similar age.

- Many unwanted babies are born with a spirit of rejection already in them. I once prayed for deliverance for a woman who had a spirit of rejection. Her mother had cruelly said to her, "I never wanted you, and I wish you had never been born." It is hard to imagine a mother saying this to her own daughter. Actually, this was such a hurtful thing to this woman that even after she received the Lord into her heart and became a Christian, she still needed deliverance.

Another time I was praying together with a pastor for a woman who was manifesting a demon. We prayed for some time but she was not getting delivered. We talked with her and she asked us if we could pray against a spirit of death. She then told us that when her mother was pregnant with her she had decided that she did not want her daughter. Consequently, the mother tried to have an abortion that did not work. It was at this time, while she was still in the womb, that the spirit of death entered. We prayed again and she was delivered from this spirit, which resulted in a wonderful change in her life.

In God's sight when a woman has an abortion she is committing murder. This can result in opening herself up to a spirit of death. On one occasion a woman came to my wife for prayer as she had been married for five years and could not have children. She had become pregnant on her honeymoon but had an abortion. After she confessed her sin as murder and asked God's forgiveness, my wife cast out the spirit of murder and the woman was delivered. Shortly afterwards, she became pregnant and now has two lovely daughters.

- If a home is full of love, joy, and worship, the presence of God will come. However, if there is swearing, fighting, and bitterness, this invites the presence of evil spirits. The negative influence of demons can often be traced to a person's terrible, abusive home life as a child. Children can have demons of hate, anger, fear, rebellion, lust, and sometimes suicide.

I once prayed for an Indian woman who had a terrible home life and had been sexually abused as a child. Her family members were idol worshippers. Even though she became a Christian, she was still troubled by evil spirits. When I came against the evil spirits within her and commanded them to come out, she fell to the floor with a piercing scream and slithered like a snake. It was a tremendous struggle, but she was wonderfully set free. She then destroyed everything in her possession associated with idolatry and the occult. Her life was completely transformed and she grew strong in the Lord and is still serving Him today.

- Emotional shock can also open a person up to demonic forces. Therefore, it is not always our own sin or even the sins of our ancestors that opens the way for an evil spirit to enter. For example, if a person was in a car accident where someone died, a spirit of fear can sometimes enter into that person. In this case, no sin was committed, but the way had been opened up for a spirit of fear to enter.

A spirit of lust is another strong spirit that can enter a person who has not flagrantly sinned in this area. An example of this is when we prayed for a nine-year-old girl who had been sexually abused by eight different men. She had actually done no sin herself, but as the victim, a spirit of lust and uncleanness had come into her. When we prayed, however, God did a wonderful work and she was completely delivered.

- A major reason that demons gain access to people is because of their own sin. For example, if you were involved in the occult before you were saved, you may need deliverance from a spirit of witchcraft. Repeated acts of wrongdoing can also open you up to demonic powers. For instance, if you continually lie, you can open yourself up to a lying spirit that will eventually come in and control you. It is the same with stealing and other sins such as anger, masturbation, fornication (sex before marriage), adultery, pornography, lust, drugs, and gluttony.

You must be especially aware of the dangers of sexual sin. God created sex, and He intended it to be a beautiful expression of love between husband and wife. Since we are a triune being, there is a joining of body, soul, and spirit of two people; they become one. When a couple engage in sex before marriage, there can be a transferring of evil spirits from one to the other.

Previously, you may have lived according to the world's standards, but now as a Christian you need to understand God's uncompromising standards of holiness. *"For this is the will of God, even your sanctification, that ye should abstain from fornication"* (1 Thess. 4:3).

- You need to be careful of the words that you speak, since wrong words can open the door to demons. Scripture tells us in Proverbs 18:21: *"Death and life are in the power of the tongue..."* For instance, in times of discouragement a person may say, "I wish I were dead!" However, words like this said too often can at times become a direct invitation for a spirit of death to enter.

HOW DO YOU GET DELIVERED?

When Jesus died on the cross, He paid the full and final penalty for all your sins. Therefore, the sacrifice of Jesus on your behalf is the basis on which you can claim full release from every demonic force the enemy has sent against you. If you are in need of deliverance in some area of your life, seek ministry from your pastor or someone experienced in deliverance. If this is not possible, you may pray yourself and cry out for God to deliver you. Joel 2:32 confirms this truth when it says, *"And it shall come to pass that whosoever shall call upon the name of the Lord shall be delivered."*

AS YOU PRAY, COVER THE FOLLOWING POINTS:

- **Affirm your faith in Christ:**

Pray a prayer something like this: "Lord Jesus I thank You that You are my Savior, and that You died on the cross for me and rose from the dead. I acknowledge You as the Lord of my life and thank You that You are my deliverer."

- **Humble yourself:**

In 1 Peter 5:5-6, we are told that God resists the proud but gives grace to the humble. Therefore, as a new believer it is essential for you to humble yourself before God. Some people say that they want to be delivered, but quietly – without any manifestation. If holding on to your dignity is more important than your deliverance, you have not really repented of pride and you therefore need to humble yourself. Thus when you pray, say something like this: "Lord, I renounce all pride and religious self-righteousness; I humble myself before You."

- **Confess any known sin and the sins of your ancestors:**

Be honest before God and acknowledge specific sins that are causing problems in your life. For example, gossip, jealousy, anger, hatred, lust, gluttony, and lying must all be confessed before God. First John 1:9 tells us: *"If we confess our sins He is faithful and just to forgive us our sins and to cleanse us from all unrighteousness."* The sins of your ancestors do not make you guilty, but they can cause you to suffer from their consequences, especially in the areas of the occult, idolatry, and immorality. As you pray, you can say something like this: "I confess all my sins Lord Jesus. Especially I confess…! I also confess and renounce all the sins of my ancestors, especially…!"

- **Repent of all your sins:**

It is important to confess your sins, but repentance is more than confessing. Repentance means that you are truly sorry for your sins and willing to forsake them. Proverbs 28:13 tells us, *"He who covers his sins will not prosper; but whosoever confesses and forsakes them will have mercy"* (NKJV). To forsake your sins means to be willing to turn away from them completely. You need to ask the Lord to help you to hate that sin even as He hates it. Therefore, you should pray something like this: "Lord, I repent of all my sins. I am truly sorry, and with your help I forsake every sin. I turn to You, Lord, for mercy and forgiveness."

- **Forgive all those who have hurt or wounded you:**

Jesus made it very clear that if you desire forgiveness from God for your sins that you must unconditionally forgive those who have sinned against you. Mark 11:25 says, *"And when ye stand praying, forgive, if ye have ought against any: that your Father also which is in heaven may forgive you your trespasses. But if ye do not forgive, neither will your Father which is in heaven forgive your trespasses."* Forgiving another person is not primarily an emotion, but it is a decision of your will. Therefore, you can pray: "By a decision of my will I choose to forgive all who have hurt me or wronged me. I lay down all bitterness and all hatred. Specifically, I forgive…!"

- **Break with the occult and every false religion:**

If you want to draw near to God, you must sever all contact with Satan. Remove from your possession anything that links you to the occult or to the Satanic realm such things as books, souvenirs, charms, idols, and objects of art associated with the occult or false religions. Moses warned Israel in Deuteronomy 7:26: *"Neither shalt thou bring an abomination into thine house, lest thou be a cursed thing like it: but thou shalt utterly detest it, and thou shalt utterly abhor it; for it is a cursed thing."* Pray something similar to this: "Lord, I sever all contact I have had with the occult or with any false religion, particularly…! I commit myself to getting rid of all objects associated with the occult or false religions.

- **Prepare to be released from every curse over your life:**

The Bible speaks about the power of blessings and curses. A curse is like a dark shadow over your life that shuts out at least part of God's blessings. Some problems that often indicate that a curse is at work in your life are mental or emotional breakdown, repeated or chronic sickness, barrenness, a breakdown in your marriage, being accident prone, and continuing financial insufficiency. However, Galatians 3:13 gives us hope as it says, *"Christ has redeemed us from the curse of the law being made a curse for us."* Therefore, it is good to pray like this: "Lord Jesus, I thank you that on the cross you were made a curse that I might be redeemed from every curse and thereby inherit God's blessing. I ask you to release me and set me free to receive the deliverance I need."

- **Take your stand with God:**

Make a firm decision and speak it out. Submit your will and your whole life to God. Make your stand with God against all sin, all evil, and every kind of demon. If the Holy Spirit gives you a name of a particular demon, verbalize it. The Bible says in James 4:7: *"Submit yourselves therefore to God. Resist the devil and he will flee from you."* As you resist him, it is good to pray something like this: "I take my stand with You, Lord, against all Satan's demons. I submit to You, and I resist the devil."

- **Expel the demon:**

When you speak in the name of Jesus, you have authority over demons. Thus, you should pray something like this: "Now I speak to any demons that have control over me, (mention their name or names if you know them) and I command you to leave me now. In the name of Jesus, I cast you out! Come out in Jesus' name!" Begin to breathe out, as demons usually leave the body through the mouth. In the Hebrew and Greek language, the word for "spirit" is the same as the word for "wind," and also for the word "breath." The way you release your breath is by expelling it through your mouth. Therefore, in the same manner you will do this when expelling a demon. As we have already said, there may be different manifestations as a demon emerges. They may come out silently or with just a little sigh or yawn. However, when I have prayed for people I have also experienced demons coming out with sobbing, crying, groaning, roaring, screaming, and also vomiting.

HOW TO KEEP YOUR DELIVERANCE

The Lord not only wants you to receive deliverance, but He wants you to stay delivered. It is one thing to be set free, but by the grace of God He wants you to stay free! As Paul said in Ephesians 4:27, *"Neither give place to the devil."* Since you do not want to give any opportunity for the demon to come back again, you must learn to shut the door so that he cannot regain an entrance back into your life. Therefore, once the enemy has been driven out, you must immediately begin to build up your walls of protection. Some ways that you can protect yourself are as follows.

1.) DEDICATE YOUR LIFE COMPLETELY TO CHRIST: Demons are extremely persistent. After being driven out, a demon may still seek to force its way back in again and even bring other demons with him. Jesus warns us of this in Matthew 12:43-45: *"When the unclean spirit is gone out of a man, he walketh through dry places, seeking rest, and findeth none. Then he saith, I will return into my house from whence I came out; and when he is come, he findeth it empty, swept, and garnished. Then goeth he, and taketh with himself seven other spirits more wicked than himself, and they enter in and dwell there: and the last state of that man is worse than the first. Even so shall it be also unto this wicked generation."*

Here the unclean spirit returned to its house or the person it formerly occupied. The problem was that the house was empty, for the man had left his house vacant through neglect. Likewise, a person who has never dedicated his life completely to the Lordship of Jesus Christ could experience this same scenario. When Jesus is the Lord of your life, you can look to Him for supernatural power to keep demons out of your spiritual house. However, without Jesus as your Lord, you do not have the strength to protect your "house." Therefore, you end up worse than you were before deliverance. Remember that you are not your own and you have been purchased by the precious blood of Christ; so make Him Lord of every area of your life.

2.) BE BAPTIZED IN WATER:

If you have never been baptized by immersion as a believer, this is an important step you need to take (see Chapter Four).

3.) BE BAPTIZED IN THE HOLY SPIRIT:

As you are baptized in the Holy Spirit and are then continuously filled with the Holy Spirit, demons will not be able to find any vacant area in your life that they can occupy (see Chapter Six).

4.) LIVE BY GOD'S WORD:

After the baptism of Jesus, He was led by the Spirit into the wilderness to be tempted by the Devil. To each temptation of the Devil, Jesus responded by quoting the Word of God. Three times Jesus said, *"It is written..."* (Matt. 4:4,7,10). Jesus used the Word of God as a weapon of attack against the enemy. Therefore, as you read the Word, think the Word, study the Word, meditate upon the Word, and act the Word—you will also have victory over the Devil and his demons. You will prosper if you heed the directions that God gave to Joshua as he was about to enter the Promised Land. *"This book of the law shall not depart out of thy mouth; but thou shalt meditate therein day and night, that thou mayest observe to do according to all that is written therein: for then thou shalt make thy way prosperous, and then thou shalt have good success"* (Josh. 1:8).

5.) PUT ON THE GARMENT OF PRAISE:

The Devil and his demons hate our praising the Lord. In Isaiah 61:3 the Lord tells us to put on *"the garment of praise"* in place of *"the spirit of heaviness."* As you learn to develop a lifestyle of praise regardless of your circumstances, demons will have to flee. When you praise the Lord, it prepares the way for the presence of God to come and greatly trouble the enemy.

In Summary:

- Jesus desires, and has the authority, to break all your bondages (John 8:36).
- Jesus gives us the same power and authority to cast out demons (Mark 16:17).
- Many Christians need deliverance from evil spirits.
- Demons desire a body to inhabit.
- Some sicknesses are caused by demons.
- We can inherit evil spirits due to the sins of our ancestors (Ex. 20:3-5).
- Beware of the dangers of sexual sin.
- Be careful of the words you speak which produce life or death.
- Always forgive others.

Recommended Reading for Further Study:

Angels
by Dr. Brian J. Bailey
Zion Christian Publishers

They Shall Expel Demons
by Dr. Derek Prince
Published by Chosen Books, a division of Baker Book House Company
P.O. Box 6287, Grand Rapids, MI 49516-6287

Chapter Six

Baptism in the Holy Spirit

A BLESSED EXPERIENCE

The wonderful and blessed experience of the baptism in the Holy Spirit can be likened to a doorway into the supernatural realm of God. It is also the key to knowing the Holy Spirit (the third Person of the Trinity) in a deeper way, and coming into the gifts of the Holy Spirit and all His wonderful blessings. This experience of the baptism in the Holy Spirit was first seen in the early Church, and this experience was that which equipped the early Christians with the miraculous power of God, enabling them to fulfill His commandments. In a very true sense, it was like the rocket that launched the early Church.

Many Christians question how this experience is relevant to us in our day, while others declare emphatically that the baptism in the Holy Spirit was only for the early Church. You can be assured that this is not so! We are living in a very serious, yet exciting time in the history of mankind. God is preparing His Church for the greatest revival and outpouring of the Holy Spirit this world has ever seen. To be a part of this great move of God it is essential to receive the baptism in the Holy Spirit. Through this experience, your spiritual senses will be awakened, and you will receive the power to be a bold witness for Christ as well as be led by the Holy Spirit.

IT IS FOR THE NEW CHRISTIAN

It is important to realize that the baptism in the Holy Spirit is not just for the mature believer. Therefore, when you receive the baptism, do not look at it as a sign from God that you are mature. Rather it is given so that you can go on to spiritual maturity. Receiving the baptism in the Holy Spirit also does not mean that you have "arrived" or that you should think of yourself as someone who has now become holy. It is simply a necessary experience to help you go on to true holiness. As a new believer, it is a wonderful experience that God has promised you; and therefore you should desire it with your whole heart.

On the day of Pentecost as the Apostle Peter preached an anointed message under the power of the Holy Spirit, the people were convicted of their sins and they cried out: *"What shall we do?"* (Acts 2:37). Peter replied, *"Repent and be baptized...and you shall receive the gift of the Holy Spirit"* (Acts 2:38). Therefore, in order to receive the baptism in the Holy Spirit, you must first repent and know you are truly saved. It is also important to be baptized in water, which is a step of obedience. Acts 5:32 says, *"And we are his witnesses of these things; and so is also the Holy Spirit, whom God has given to them that obey him."* There are some exceptions when God chooses to baptize people in the Holy Spirit before they are baptized in water (like Cornelius and his household in Acts 10), but generally most people are baptized in water first before receiving the Holy Spirit of God.

PROMISED IN THE OLD TESTAMENT

The outpouring of the Holy Spirit spoken of by the prophet Joel (Joel 2:28) also speaks of the experience of the baptism in the Holy Spirit. *"And it shall come to pass afterward that I will pour out my spirit upon all flesh; and your sons and your daughters shall prophesy, your old men shall dream dreams, your young men shall see visions."* Peter refers to this verse on the day of Pentecost, saying that the baptism in the Holy Spirit was a part of the fulfillment of the prophecy of Joel (Acts 2:16-17). The Holy Spirit was first prophesied about in the Old Testament, but was first experienced on the day of Pentecost (Acts 2:1-4).

Just before Jesus ascended into heaven, He gave his disciples clear instructions to wait in Jerusalem for *"the promise of the father"* (Acts 1:4). Isaiah 44:3 reveals the promise that the Father made to His Son Jesus, *"For I will pour water upon him that is thirsty, and floods upon the dry ground: I will pour my spirit upon thy seed, and my blessing upon thine offspring."*

Here the Father promised the Son that He would pour out His Spirit upon His seed, which are all those who believe and are truly saved. On the day of Pentecost, Peter also referred to this "promise of the Holy Spirit" by God the Father. *"Therefore being by the right hand of God exalted, and having received of the Father the promise of the Holy Spirit, he has shed forth this, which ye now see and hear"* (Acts 2:33).

We read about this "promise" again in Acts 2:39: *"For the promise is unto you, and to your children, and to all that are afar off, even as many as the Lord our God shall call."* So, as you can see from this Scripture, the wonderful promise of the baptism in the Holy Spirit is not only for us, but for our children as well.

BIBLE PHRASES THAT DESCRIBE THE BAPTISM IN THE HOLY SPIRIT

1.) Baptized with the Holy Spirit:

In Acts 1:5 we are given this phrase: *"For John truly baptized with water, but you shall be baptized with the Holy Spirit not many days from now."* As we have previously said, the word "baptism" means a complete immersion. Therefore, being baptized with the Holy Spirit means that you are immersed in the Holy Spirit.

2.) Filled with the Holy Spirit:

When you are saved and "born again," you have the Holy Spirit (Rom. 8:9), but there is a difference between *having* the Holy Spirit and *being filled* with the Holy Spirit. On the day of Pentecost, we see that they were all filled with the Holy Spirit. *"And they were all filled with the Holy Spirit and began to speak with other tongues, as the Spirit gave them utterance"* (Acts 2:4).

3.) Receive the gift of the Holy Spirit:
Peter speaks of this experience in Acts 2:38 as something we receive from God. *"Repent and be baptized ...and you shall receive the gift of the Holy Spirit"* (Acts 2:38).

4.) The Holy Ghost fell on them:
In Acts 10:44 we read: *"While Peter yet spoke these words, the Holy Spirit fell on all them which heard the word."*

5.) Poured out the gift of the Holy Spirit:
Here again is the thought of the Holy Spirit coming upon you. For Acts 10:45 tells us, *"And they of the circumcision which believed were astonished, as many as came with Peter, because that on the Gentiles also was poured out the gift of the Holy Spirit."*

6.) Endued with power from on high:
Shortly before Jesus ascended into heaven, He instructed the disciples to wait in Jerusalem until they were endued (or clothed upon) with power from on high. *"And, behold, I send the promise of my Father upon you: but tarry ye in the city of Jerusalem, until ye be endued with power from on high"* (Luke 24:49).

THE BAPTISM IN THE HOLY SPIRIT AS A SECOND EXPERIENCE

Receiving the baptism in the Holy Spirit is not salvation or being born again, but is a definite, separate experience that follows your salvation. This is clearly seen in the Old Testament in the Feasts of the Lord.

The Feast of Passover was celebrated to commemorate the children of Israel coming out of Egypt. We find in Exodus 12, just before God brought them out of Egypt, each family was instructed by God to kill a lamb on the fourteenth day of the first month and apply the blood to the doorposts and lintels of their houses. Then when the death angel passed over the land, the firstborn in every Egyptian household died, but the Israelites who had the blood of the lamb on their houses were saved and no one died.

This Feast of Passover was fulfilled when Jesus *"the Lamb of God"* died on the cross at Calvary for our sins. Therefore, in a personal way, you experienced this Feast spiritually when you repented of your sins, received Christ into your heart as your Savior, and were wonderfully saved through His blood that was shed for you.

The Old Testament Feast of Pentecost was in the third month, when the children of Israel had come to Mt. Sinai in the wilderness. It was exactly fifty days after they had crossed over the Red Sea on dry land. This Feast, which was spiritually fulfilled on the day of Pentecost, was exactly fifty days after Jesus rose from the dead. *"And when the day of Pentecost was fully come, they were all with one accord in one place. And suddenly there came a sound from heaven as of a rushing mighty wind, and it filled all the house where they were sitting. And there appeared unto them cloven tongues like as of fire, and it sat upon each of them. And they were all filled with the Holy Ghost, and began to speak with other tongues, as the Spirit gave them utterance"* (Acts 2:1-4). Therefore, in a personal way, you spiritually experience the Feast of Pentecost when you receive the baptism in the Holy Spirit.

In the same way that the Feast of Passover and the Feast of Pentecost were two separate feasts in the Old Testament, so also are being saved and being baptized in the Holy Spirit two separate experiences. In Acts 8:4-17 we read the account of Philip going to Samaria, and as he preached the Word of God, revival broke out. Many people turned from paganism to Jesus Christ; there were miracles and healings that accompanied the preaching of the Word. Many were delivered from evil spirits and the new converts were baptized in water.

Yet when news of this great revival reached the apostles in Jerusalem, they were concerned that the new believers had not received the baptism in the Holy Spirit. Consequently, they sent Peter and John to Samaria to lay hands on the new converts and pray that they might be baptized in the Holy Spirit. *"Who, when they were come down, prayed for them, that they might receive the Holy Ghost: (For as yet he was fallen upon none of them: only they were baptized in the name of the Lord Jesus.) Then laid they their hands on them, and they received the Holy Ghost"* (Acts 8:15-17). When Peter and John prayed for them to receive the baptism in the Holy Spirit it was obviously some time after their salvation. However, in the case of Cornelius and his household (Acts Chapter 10), we see that they were saved and baptized in the Holy Spirit at the same time.

In Acts 19:1-8, the Apostle Paul came to Ephesus on his third missionary journey and found a small group of Jesus' disciples. Noticing something missing from their Christian experience, he asked, *"Have you received the Holy Spirit since you believed?"* (Acts 19:2). By this question, Paul is in fact emphasizing the point here that conversion is one experience and the baptism in the Holy Spirit is a separate, subsequent experience. We could restate Paul's question in a slightly different way without changing its meaning. In essence, Paul was asking the Ephesian disciples, "Have you received the baptism in the Holy Spirit since you accepted Jesus Christ as your Savior?" Paul then baptized the twelve men in water, laid hands on them, and prayed for them to receive the baptism in the Holy Spirit (Acts 19:5-7).

IT IS THE WILL OF GOD FOR EVERY BELIEVER

Scripture shows us that the baptism in the Holy Spirit is the will of God for **every** believer. As we have previously said, the Old Testament Feast of Pentecost (also called the Feast of Weeks) is a type of the baptism in the Holy Spirit. Therefore, it is important to remember that this feast was a time of rejoicing and **everyone** was included: sons, daughters, menservants, maidservants, Levites, strangers, the fatherless, and the widows (Deut. 16:10-11).

The New Testament Scriptures also confirm this same truth that the baptism is for everyone. On the day of Pentecost, Peter said in Acts 2:39: *"For the promise* (referring to the baptism in the Holy Spirit) *is unto you, and to your children, and to all that are afar off, even as many as the Lord our God shall call."* Therefore, it is very clear that this experience was for Peter's generation, for the children of that generation, and also for all those *"afar off."* But equally as important, he finishes up his statement by saying that this experience is also for *"as many as the Lord shall call."* In other words, this experience is for every believer in every generation.

In Acts 10:1-48, we see that Cornelius was one of the first Gentiles to be baptized in the Holy Spirit. This occurred about ten years after the day of Pentecost, but up until that time the Gospel had only been preached to the Jews. However, now God was showing Peter that the Holy Spirit was not just for the Jews but was for **all** people. In Acts 10:45 we read about how the Spirit was poured out upon the Gentile believers. *"And they of the circumcision* (the Jews) *which believed were astonished, as many as came with Peter, because that on the Gentiles also was poured out the* *gift of the Holy Ghost."* Therefore, as a new believer you can be absolutely sure that this glorious experience of the baptism of the Holy Spirit is for you.

THE INITIAL EVIDENCE OF THE BAPTISM IN THE HOLY SPIRIT

Central to the experience of the baptism in the Holy Spirit is the evidence of speaking in other tongues, which can be explained as the out-rushing of the Spirit of God through the believer. We do not read of anyone speaking in tongues in the Old Testament, but the Lord reserved this sign for the outpouring of the Holy Spirit on the day of Pentecost. It was an unmistakable sign which confirmed that the 120 in the upper room had received the baptism in the Holy Spirit.

Speaking in tongues (the initial sign of the baptism in the Holy Spirit) is debated and contested by many Christians. Some think they have received the baptism in the Holy Spirit without any evidence; others think they have received because they had some emotional experience like laughing, or they felt the Holy Spirit go through their body like electricity. We would agree that perhaps they were touched by the Holy Spirit in some way; however, it was not the baptism in the Holy Spirit if they did not speak in tongues.

Satan hates speaking in tongues and he will do everything he can to hinder believers from receiving this glorious experience.

Even on the day of Pentecost when the 120 people who were gathered there first began to speak in tongues, the devil tried to discredit the experience through mockers who said that these people were drunk with wine (Acts 2:13).

When you get baptized in water, something happens. Obviously, you get wet! In the same way, when you are baptized in the Holy Spirit, the initial evidence, sign, or proof that you have received is that you begin to speak with other tongues. It is therefore important to study the New Testament Scriptures that confirm this evidence. We will now examine the five cases in the book of Acts where people were baptized in the Holy Spirit.

1.) On the day of Pentecost — Acts 2:1-4:
Obeying the word of Jesus, the 120 people had been waiting in the upper room in Jerusalem for ten days before the Holy Spirit was poured out. It was on the exact day of the Jewish Feast of Pentecost. *"And they were all filled with the Holy Ghost, and began to speak with other tongues, as the Spirit gave them utterance"* (Acts 2:4). Peter also tells us in Acts 2:33, *"And having received from the Father the promise of the Holy Spirit, He poured out this which you now* ***see*** *and* ***hear****."* In other words, the Jews could see and hear the disciples speaking in other tongues.

2.) The Apostle Paul — Acts 9:17:
After the dramatic conversion of Paul on the road to Damascus, he became blind for three days. God sent Ananias to pray for

him, who then said to Paul, *"Receive thy sight and be filled with the Holy Ghost"* (Acts 9:17). In Acts, it does not specifically mention that he spoke in tongues. However, we know that he did because in 1 Corinthians 14:18 he confirms it by saying: *"I thank my God I speak with tongues more than you all"* (NKJV). In the same chapter, he also declared *"I would that you all spoke with tongues"* (v. 5, NKJV).

3.) Cornelius and his household — Acts 10:44-46:
Peter was supernaturally instructed to visit the household of Cornelius, who was a Gentile and a Roman centurion. Through this event, God was going to show Peter and the apostles that he had accepted the Gentiles. In this case, God's acceptance of them was shown when He baptized them in the Holy Spirit. *"While Peter was still speaking these words, the Holy Spirit fell upon all those who heard the word. And those of the circumcision* (the Jews) *who believed were astonished, as many as came with Peter, because the gift of the Holy Spirit had been poured out on the Gentiles also. For they heard them speak with tongues and magnify God"* (Acts 10:44-46, NKJV).

It is very clear in this account that the reason Peter and his companions knew that Cornelius and his household had been baptized in the Holy Spirit was because they heard them speak with other tongues. In addition to that, when Peter is reporting the incident to the apostles and brethren back in Jerusalem, he further confirms this truth by saying *"the Holy Ghost fell on them, as on us at the beginning"* (Acts 11:15). Obviously, Peter accepted the validity of the baptism in the Holy Spirit at Cornelius' house because they spoke in tongues in the same way the 120 had spoken in tongues about ten years earlier on the day of Pentecost.

4.) The believers at Ephesus — Acts 19:1-7:
Here in Ephesus Paul found a small group of true believers that had not yet been filled with the Holy Spirit. However, after Paul laid his hands upon them, *"the Holy Spirit came on them, and they spoke with tongues and prophesied"* (Acts 19:6, NKJV). Here again we see that they spoke in tongues, and in this case they prophesied as well.

5.) The Samaritan believers — Acts 8:5-25:
Peter and John came from Jerusalem to pray for the new Samaritan believers and they received the baptism in the Holy Spirit (Acts 8:17). On this occasion it does not specifically mention that they spoke in tongues; however, if you carefully read what happened afterwards, there was a significant outward sign. *"And when Simon saw that through the laying on of the apostles' hands the Holy Spirit was given, he offered them money, saying, "Give me this power also, that anyone on whom I lay hands may receive the Holy Spirit""* (Acts 8:18,19).

Simon the sorcerer, who was accustomed to seeing miracles, saw something that day so miraculous that when the disciples laid hands on people and they received the Holy Spirit, he was willing to pay them money for that power. Obviously, there must have been an unmistakable outward sign when these believers were baptized in the Holy Spirit. Furthermore, in light of the above four accounts, it would strongly indicate that Simon heard these people speak in other tongues.

YOU SHALL RECEIVE POWER

The main purpose of the baptism in the Holy Spirit is to receive power to be bold witnesses for Christ. Shortly before Jesus ascended into heaven He told his disciples that He would send the **promise of His Father**, and that they were to wait in Jerusalem until they were ***"endued with power from on high"*** (Luke 24:49).

In Acts 1:8 Jesus said, *"But ye shall receive power, after that the Holy Ghost is come upon you: and ye shall be witnesses unto me both in Jerusalem, and in all Judaea, and in Samaria, and unto the uttermost part of the earth."* The word that Jesus uses for "power" in this verse is the Greek word "dunamis," from which we receive the English word "dynamite." As we all know, dynamite has incredible power and can break huge, hard rocks in pieces. Another English word derived from "dunamis" is the word "dynamo." A dynamo is a machine that generates a consistent and continuing supply of power. In the same way, through the baptism of the Holy Spirit, God wants to generate within you this same supply of power in the form of supernatural strength, power, and ability to witness and live for Jesus.

The word "witnesses" in this verse is the Greek word "martus" from which we get the English word "martyr." This speaks of one who lays down his life for the Lord or is willing to do so by God's grace. Shortly before Christ was crucified, His disciples forsook Him and fled; Peter even denied Him three times. However, after the Holy Spirit came upon them on the day of Pentecost, they were changed men who had a new power and boldness they had never known before. Peter stood up with no fear or timidity, and with much boldness preached a powerful, anointed sermon—resulting in about 3,000 people coming to Christ (Acts 2:14-41). All the apostles, except for the Apostle John, later gave their lives by becoming martyrs for the sake of the Gospel.

HOW TO RECEIVE THE BAPTISM IN THE HOLY SPIRIT

People can receive the baptism in different ways and everyone's experience is unique. For example, we find in Acts that many people were filled with the Holy Spirit when someone prayed for them and laid hands upon them (Acts 8:17; 9:17; 19:6). Most people today receive this experience by the laying on of hands, but others receive when they are alone, or in some other way. Some people receive by having a great emotional experience, yet many others genuinely receive the baptism in the Holy Spirit with the evidence of speaking in tongues without any emotions at all.

After sharing the following simple instructions and praying for people, I have had the privilege of seeing the Lord baptize thousands of people in the Holy Spirit with the evidence of speaking in other tongues, in seminars, conventions, and churches in many different countries.

- **Repent:** In order for you to receive the baptism in the Holy Spirit, you must first repent and have a genuine experience of being born again (Acts 2:38, John 3:3).

- **Be baptized in Water:** In most cases in the New Testament, people were first baptized in water (see Acts 2:38). However, in some cases, such as Cornelius and his household, they were baptized in the Holy Spirit first and afterwards were baptized in water.

- **Be obedient:** Sometimes the Lord will require you to do certain acts of obedience before He will baptize you in the Holy Spirit. For example, in Acts 5:32 it says: *"And we are His witnesses to these things, and so also is the Holy Spirit whom God has given to those who **obey** Him."* On one occasion I prayed for a group of people and everyone received except one young married woman. I felt impressed of the Lord to show her this Scripture in Acts 5:32, and then I asked her to pray. Quickly, the Lord brought to her mind a situation where she had not obeyed her husband and had been deceptive. She apologized to him and put it right and then came to church the following Sunday. During praise and worship, without anyone even laying hands on her, she was filled with the Holy Spirit and spoke in other tongues.

- **The baptism in the Holy Spirit is a gift:** It is important for you to understand that the baptism in the Holy Spirit is a gift and you do not have to work for it, earn it, or lose control of yourself – just relax and receive. Peter said, *"Repent and be baptized...and you will receive the **gift** of the Holy Spirit"* (Acts 2:38, NKJV). Jesus also stated in Luke 11:13, *"If ye then, being evil, know how to give good gifts unto your children: how much more shall your heavenly Father **give** the Holy Spirit to them that ask him?"* God the Father will not give you anything evil. On the contrary, He delights to give good gifts to His children (see Luke 11:11-13).

- **Receive by faith:** You receive the baptism of the Holy Spirit by faith, not by feelings. Some may have great emotional experiences, but others will not. However, if there is unbelief in your heart, it will hinder you from receiving. When Paul wrote to the Galatians he said: *"Received ye the Spirit by the works of the law, or by the hearing of faith?"* (Gal. 3:2).

- **Jesus is the baptizer:** Jesus said in John 7:37, *"...If any man thirst, let him come unto **me**, and drink."* It is also important to realize that Jesus is the baptizer in the Holy Spirit!

You are coming to Him—not to a denomination, a church, or a preacher. When John the Baptist introduced Jesus at the time of His baptism, he introduced Him as the baptizer in the Holy Spirit: *"I indeed baptize you with water, but one mightier than I cometh...he shall baptize you with the Holy Spirit and with fire"* (Luke 3:16).

- **Desire to receive:** You must have a desire to receive. In John 7:37, Jesus said, *"If any man **thirst**."* Are you thirsty for the water of the Spirit? If you are, you may come unto Jesus and drink. Those who are hungry and thirsty will be those who are filled. Sadly, the reason that many people are not filled with the Holy Spirit is because they have no real desire to receive.

- **Drink to receive:** Do not be passive, you must drink! In John 7:37 Jesus tells us, *"If anyone thirst let him come unto me and **drink.**"* Even if you are very thirsty and water is available, your thirst will not be quenched unless you do something about it. Obviously, you must pick up the glass of water and drink. Usually in receiving the baptism in the Holy Spirit, there is your part (which is natural) and God's part (which is supernatural). In other words you must do the possible before you can expect God to do the impossible. We see an example of this when the disciples were crossing the Sea of Galilee and a terrible storm arose. Jesus came to them walking on the water and Peter cried out, *"Lord, if it is You, command me to come to You on the water"* (Matt. 14:28, NKJV). The Lord's reply to

Peter was to come, and by faith he obeyed the words of Jesus. A miracle happened and Peter began to walk on the water. However, there would have been no miracle if Peter had remained seated in the boat and done nothing. Peter had to stand up and jump over the side of the boat, then God gave him supernatural power to walk on the water.

If you keep your mouth closed you will not receive. Your part in receiving the baptism in the Holy Spirit is by faith to open your mouth and speak out the new words the Holy Spirit will give to you – using your tongue, your lips, and your voice. On the day of Pentecost, *"**They** began to speak..."* (Acts 2:4).

No one can speak in two languages at exactly the same time; so do not pray in English or in your own language. The new words may sound strange to your mind because they are unknown to you. You may begin with stammering lips or with just one or two words. Do not doubt, but speak out what the Holy Spirit brings to your mind and trust the Lord to give you more words.

As a new believer, I would encourage you to be prayed for with the laying on of hands to receive this experience, either at a church altar call or by a pastor or church leader. When I pray for people to receive the baptism in the Holy Spirit, I often ask them to pray aloud after me, and then I encourage them to begin speaking in tongues. They may pray a prayer similar to the following:

"Dear Lord Jesus, I thank you that you are my Savior and Lord. I believe that you are the baptizer in the Holy Spirit. I ask you now to baptize me in the Holy Spirit with the initial evidence of speaking in other tongues, that I might glorify You in a new language. Give me power to be a bold witness for You. I receive now by faith and I thank you Jesus."

THE ONGOING EXPERIENCE OF THE BAPTISM IN THE HOLY SPIRIT

It is wonderful to experience the baptism in the Holy Spirit, but God desires it to be a continuing experience in your life so that day by day you are filled with the Holy Spirit. As we have said previously, the meaning of baptism is to be completely immersed; therefore, God desires that you be completely immersed in the Holy Spirit so that every area of your life is filled with the presence and anointing of the Spirit.

On the day of Pentecost, the disciples were baptized in the Holy Spirit (Acts 2:4), but these same disciples were refilled in Acts 4:31. *"And when they had prayed, the place where they were assembled together was shaken; and they were all filled with the Holy Spirit, and they spoke the word of God with boldness."* Another Scripture that bears out this truth is found in Ephesians 5:18: *"And be not drunk with wine, wherein is excess; but **be filled with the Spirit**."*

Paul is not talking here about the initial experience of the baptism in the Holy Spirit but the ongoing experience. The words *"be filled"* are in the present continuous tense and the meaning in Greek is "to be filled and keep on being filled" with the Holy Spirit.

For instance, a car's oil level must be checked periodically. If the engine is low in oil, you must then pour in more oil in order to "fill up" to the correct level. Likewise, you need to be filled afresh or refilled with the Holy Spirit. By His grace, you need to be continually filled with the Holy Spirit so that there is an overflow of His life in your life.

In Ephesians 5:19 Paul gives us a key on how to keep being filled with the Holy Spirit: *"Speaking to yourselves in psalms and hymns and spiritual songs, singing and making melody in your heart to the Lord."* You are to sing spiritual songs to yourself and also sing in other tongues.

A vital key to keeping filled with the Holy Spirit is to daily pray in other tongues. Even though you cannot understand the words you are praying, the Bible says that when you pray in tongues you are not praying to men but to God, and you are building yourself up spiritually (1 Cor. 14:2,4). You should pray in tongues not only in your prayer times or at church, but also at other times such as while cleaning the house, washing dishes, driving a car, or doing other duties. The Apostle Paul, who was constantly filled with the Holy Spirit and mightily used of God, was able to say, *"I thank my God, I speak with tongues more than you all"* (1 Cor. 14:18).

In Summary:

- In order to receive the baptism in the Holy Spirit, you must repent and be saved.
- In the Old Testament, the term "the Promise of the Father" refers to this experience.
- The baptism in the Holy Spirit is a second definite experience, subsequent to salvation.
- The baptism in the Holy Spirit was not just given to the early Church; it is for all believers.
- The Holy Spirit is freely given to all who are thirsty.
- The initial sign that you have received the baptism in the Holy Spirit is that you speak in tongues.
- The main purpose of the baptism of the Holy Spirit is to receive power to be bold witnesses for Christ.
- After receiving this experience, it is important to continue to be filled with the Holy Spirit.

Recommended Reading for Further Study:

The Comforter
by Dr. Brian J. Bailey
Zion Christian Publishers

IN CONCLUSION

We have now come to the end of our study, and I would like to stress a few important points. God intended your Christian life to be an exciting, fulfilling, challenging, and lively pursuit of perfection in Christ. The Christian life is an active life of seeking to be conformed to the image of Christ and pressing toward the mark of the high calling of God in Christ Jesus. Therefore, the power and inspiration of this meaningful Christian life is embodied in a living person—Jesus Christ. He is the reason that we live, and move, and have our being. It is only in Him and through Him that we have a purposeful life.

Before Christ came into our lives, we were nothing—hopelessly lost and terribly alone in our sin until He picked us up and saved us. Jesus died for us, and therefore, we owe Him our lives. We were purchased by His blood and bought with a price, therefore we are no longer our own. This is indeed the simplicity of the Gospel of Christ. We are no longer free to live our life just any way we wish to live it. For now we belong to another to whom we must pledge our allegiance, and to whom we must look to for guidance and direction, faithfully following wherever He may lead.

God does not expect us to pursue Him without His help and guidance. He does not want us to go through this journey alone, nor does He expect us to fight life's battles without Him. His Word tells us that He will never leave us or forsake us. In His Word, He also gives us the rules of this life, even as He exemplifies these rules through His own life. God's Word makes it clear that we are to be holy as He is holy, perfect as He is perfect, merciful as He is merciful, and so forth.

Consequently, the reason we have written this handbook is that you, as a new believer, may find answers to questions that you may have since you made the decision to give your life to the Lord. God's desire is to grant you understanding of His ways, and we trust that this book will provide for you vital keys to open up your understanding. Therefore, as you are learning what it means to be a believer, we encourage you to use this handbook as a teaching guide and a companion book to your Bible. By God's grace we pray that this ***Handbook for New Believers*** will inspire you to continue fervently seeking Him with your whole heart. For surely, He is worthy!